The 4th Competitive Force For Good

ESG Leadership and Efficient and Effective Cybersecurity

Hendrik J Troskie

PARTRIDGE

ISBN:	Hardcover	978-1-5437-5939-6
	Softcover	978-1-5437-5937-2
	eBook	978-1-5437-5938-9

To order additional copies of this book, contact
Toll Free +65 3165 7531 (Singapore)
Toll Free +60 3 3099 4412 (Malaysia)
orders.singapore@partridgepublishing.com

www.partridgepublishing.com/singapore

To Louise
There is a better way.

CONTENTS

FIGURES

INTRODUCTION

The 4ᵗʰ Competitive Force for Good

How to Manage Corporate Cybersecurity by using Environment, Social and Governance (ESG) Frameworks to Achieve Risk Reduction and Cut the Cost of Cybersecurity

Introduction:

Imagine the world having US$6 trillion every year, without the need to borrow from future generations or dig into reserves. Imagine what the world could do with that money in its fight against the Coronavirus and the disease it causes, Covid-19.

In fact, imagine US$6 trillion invested in the global healthcare industry every year to prepare for and to deal with novel viruses. Imagine the stockpile of PPEs, ventilators, ICUs, and armies of medical practitioners that it can pay for.

US$6 trillion is what the global economy will lose from cybercrime by 2021[1]. Losses already amount to US$3 trillion per annum and is facing an exponential growth. Cybercrime is not just about the posterchild hacks, the billion-dollar hacks that make the frontpages. It affects everybody, from the retirees who see their life savings stolen by online scammers, small and medium size businesses that close their doors following ransomware attacks. Every individual carries this burden.

Cybercrime is such a growing threat to individuals, businesses and institutions - and the global community - that the World Economic Forum Global Risk Report 2019 rates cyberattacks second only to the climate emergency. Both risks are man-made, and both are caused – in the opinion of this author - by an unfettered exploitation by business of science and technology for a profit.

> "Technology continues to play a profound role in shaping the global risks landscape. Concerns about data fraud and cyber-attacks were prominent again in the Global Risks Perception Survey(GRPS), which also highlighted a number of other **technological vulnerabilities**: around two-thirds of respondents expect the risks associated with fake news and identity theft to increase in 2019, while three-fifths said the same about loss of privacy to companies and governments. There were further massive data breaches in 2018, new hardware weaknesses were revealed, and research pointed to the potential uses of artificial intelligence to engineer more potent cyber- attacks. Last year also provided further evidence that cyber-attacks pose risks to critical infrastructure, prompting countries to strengthen their screening of cross-border partnerships on national security grounds."

Extract WEF 2019

A virus like SARS-Cov-2 that causes the disease COVID-19 is a natural phenomenon, one of billions, some of which will jump species at some point. Much can be done to research predict and prepare for virus infections. In contrast, cybercrime is an entirely man-made phenomenon. It's not naturally there.

Cybercrime is there because of the way society is organised around business, the economy, and politics.

US$6 trillion of losses is the future that is already here. It is an almost inevitable consequence of what we have already done. Businesses have created a global information infrastructure that for all the value it brings is riddled with weaknesses, is fragile and easily subverted. There is little we can do now but brace ourselves for the high probability of the inevitable losses.

But there is also the problem of possibilities. The possibility that nation states will target the information infrastructure as a means to settle geopolitical tensions. This is already happening. It is just not evenly distributed.

The collapse of the information ecosystem[2] is as plausible as SARS-Cov-2 jumping species. The COVID-19 Pandemic has exposed the global community's lack of preparedness to deal with global infections. It is only a matter of time that an attack on the information ecosystem will expose the same lack of preparedness by businesses to deal with a major cyberattack.

Let us clarify what is meant by **cybersecurity**. It is not always clear. In some circles it is about cybersecurity related to information technology. It stands in a way apart from *information security* which is about the security of all forms of information, verbal, telephone, and hardcopy printed format. As such **cybersecurity** is a subset of *information security*.

However, this view is disrespectful to the etymology of the word cyber. Cyber is the prefix to the term cybernetics which is the study of the system that governs through information. The suffix, 'netics' means to study which suggests the prefix 'cyber', means the system that governs through information. This interpretation makes it compatible with what gave rise to the word cybernetics in the first place.

Cybernetics is derived from Kubernetes; a reference to the helmsman of an ancient Greek ship, a trireme. It was used by Socrates to explain to Alcibiades something much more complicated than simply the person in control of the rudder. Socrates explained that a Kubernetes steered the vessel by issuing instructions to the sometimes hundreds of rowers on three decks of the trireme. Hence, a Kubernetes steered the vessel through *information* and must have the required expertise to be able do that.

Later the word Kubernetes gave rise to the word government and specifically the meaning to govern through information. Governments issue laws and policies in the official government gazette which are acts of transmitting information in order to govern. By adopting the term cyber to mean systems that govern through information we derive a clearer understanding of what is meant by related terms:

- A cyberattack is to attack the system that governs through information in order to harm the system.
- Cybercrime is to subvert the system that governs through information to steal something of value.
- Cyberwar is to attack a nation states information infrastructure to interrupt its social systems.
- Cybersecurity is the protection of the system that governs through information.
- Cyberdefence is the defence of the system that govern through information.

It matters not what medium is used to communicate the information, whether paper documents, conversations or information and communication technology. It is information in its various forms that governs the activity of all employees of a business and their interaction with the rest of society, supplier, customers, investors and each other. This meaning collapses the distinction between information security and cybersecurity and is the meaning that will carry forward in this book. The distinction between information security and cybersecurity carried little merit anyway.

We can now consider a business as an organisation that is governed through information, but what information? There is a certain absence of academic rigour in business. It seems that just about everyone can coin a new phrase or new term to encapsulate a new creative management or leadership process. But we can only have a meaningful discussion if we clarify what is meant by business. In this enquiry we consider a business to be a theory.

Starting with its business plan, mission or purpose as the theory that drives the business which combines with many other theories to build a working system governed through information. Other theories might be financial management, cost accounting, procurement, human resources, sales and marketing, design and engineering and many more. Employees of the business execute the methodology and methods of the theory in order to make the business a reality. The methodologies and methods of the theory defines the information that governs the business.

Similarly, the economy like a business follow a theory or combinations of theories. For instance, a country can follow the capitalist, Marxist, communist or socialist market theories, or a combination of those in the way a society is organised for commerce. Take the UK for instance. It follows a largely Marxist market theory for its healthcare services, but a capitalist market theory for almost everything else, except for employment regulation where it follows a more or less socialist market theory.

So, I propose to take forward the view that a business is a theory first which in turn is a combination of many other theories that combine in a system governed through information to execute its purpose. I will revert to standard business language in discussing functions, operational units, departments or business units, but always keep in mind that these are theories with processes and tasks executed by humans and machines to combine to build the business. The importance of this approach will become clear later. Using the understanding that cyber is about governance through information puts into sharp focus the importance and the recognition of a need for *security in information,* which in some circles is referred to as *technology governance.* That is what we will focus much more of our attention on in the course of this work.

* * *

So why am I attempting to produce some sort of recipe or management process for dealing with cybersecurity in the context that it means to secure systems that govern through information?

Over the last ten years or so, I have worked with businesses of every kind, probably within every industry, on the problems associated with *cybersecurity.* Some really great companies definitely demonstrate frictionless cybersecurity management.

On the other hand, I've observed some companies at the opposite end of that spectrum.

There are some companies that rarely ask for a gap assessment against a framework of choice yet still have great cybersecurity.

Then there are those that repeatedly perform annual gap assessments with different consulting firms, which are followed by remediation programmes that don't quite deliver on the promise. And the process is repeated year after year, but sadly, with little progress made.

The typical way of convincing customers to take up a consultancy programme is to reference the successful track records of high-achieving consultants. But I have worked with cybersecurity transformation consultants who did great work and made a real difference, but who were frequently unable to articulate precisely why they were successful.

No one seemed able to present a case based on theory, methodology and method. As such, the business case rarely stacked up. Investment requirements were vague and ambiguous. The customer was often left feeling inadequate and ill-equipped to deal with the problem themselves.

Thus, having failed to make a convincing business case, consultancies resort to injecting fear, uncertainty, and doubt, citing recent posterchild hacks and related financial losses to persuade potential clients to invest in cybersecurity management consulting services. Alternatively, consultancies cite case studies of past successes which are not commensurate with the business they're soliciting. It is a myth that history repeats itself. The case studies and past successes occurred within a context that is out of proportion for the business considering the service. There is no guarantee that past successes will bring about future successes in a different context.

All of this fired up a curiosity that prompted me to research this problem more fully and to consider writing about it.

I started out with the intention of producing a white paper, but as it grew and went through the editing process, I saw the need to build the case for change more robustly.

I need to be transparent about the methodology. I could have researched data, reports and assessments, conducted many interviews and analysed piles of statistics. But this has been done before and the results offered no clear answer. In fact, their conclusions invariably boil down to 'You must create the right cybersecurity culture.'

But this does not pass philosophical scrutiny. Culture is epiphenomenal. It arises from the values of a business and cannot be fixed.

Culture shifts in response to changes in management, the wider workforce and across geographical regions. Culture is not a tangible thing; hence you cannot conjure up a great culture and impose it onto a business. And a business culture built up in one big geography cannot automatically be transplanted elsewhere around the world.

I realised there had to be another way to analyse and examine the problem. The methodology I decided on was to identify *business management theories* that had found their way into the boardroom, then assemble the methodologies and methods into the control systems used in business.

Finally, I assess how the control systems can work together and reveal the unintended consequences they produce. At times, I reference supporting facts that are easily accessible on the internet, but I suggest the reader explores the bibliography for a more complete understanding of the theories I use and propose as a solution. I kept my review of many of the theories to the bare minimum so as not to create burdensome reading.

In the course of my study, research and writing, I kept coming up against the subject of sustainability, which I found to be in the foreground of any discourse in business these days. It's of interest to note that Sustainability Reporting is a requirement for listed companies in most jurisdictions around the world, and for many Multi-National Corporations (MNCs) seen to be as important as Financial Reporting. You only have to look at the Dow Jones Sustainability Indices to realise how seriously major corporations take sustainability.

The focus on sustainability for business is very much on environmental factors and in particular on the use or otherwise of carbon-based fossil fuel energy. And so it should be. The world is facing a climate emergency. Remember, that by the World Economic Forum ratings, the climate emergency is just ahead of cyberattacks as among the biggest risks faced by business globally.

Sustainability issues, when focussed on, have given rise to purposeful businesses. With sustainability, there is an increasing focus on the business to be a force for good in society as well: businesses that are focused on a social purpose, not just on making profit.

It was some time back that John Elkington coined the phrase Triple Bottom Line (TBL) - covering People, Planet and Profit - in his landmark 1997 book *Cannibals with Forks: the Triple Bottom Line of 21st Century Business*. Many organizations have adopted the TBL framework to evaluate their performance in a broader perspective to create greater business value.

This is not to downplay profit, which remains a vital aspect for any business. But businesses that follow the TBL, or even better, the Environment, Social and Governance (ESG) framework, are increasingly performing better than businesses that don't.

It has been observed that ESG businesses enjoy significantly less intervention from regulators and can access opportunities and markets with less red tape and less resistance from the public. This means that they are better for their shareholders, better for society *and* better for the environment.

So when we seriously look into all this, we see that the root cause of the growing cyber threat lies in the midst of the very same problems that are being successfully addressed by the ESG framework: the relentless application of business thinking (Business case, ROI, Cost-Benefit Analysis, etc.) and the single-minded focus on science to solve these problems.

This book therefore explores the theories, methodologies and methods used in ESG businesses' decision-making and shows how changing to a more ethical business model reduces costs, increases market share, and increases investor returns.

It goes on to examine the fit between cybersecurity and ESG frameworks, concluding that cybersecurity is fundamentally a social and governance issue and thus a human issue, with undeniable ethical and moral implications.

This enquiry reveals the root cause behind the cybersecurity problem, which is a consequence of the application of misinformed theories for organisational design and a single-minded pursuit of profit. It then proposes that business can *significantly reduce the cost of cybersecurity risk management*, whilst reaching *a higher level of effective risk reduction* by applying the same ESG management methodologies.

So back to the major twin issues at the top of the WEF Global Risk table. The Climate Emergency and Cyberattacks. Both risks are man-made, and both brought about by an unfettered exploitation by business of science and technology for a profit.

So, make no mistake. This book is definitely about the problem of managing cybersecurity. But I need to point out that the underpinning problem existed in business management before cybersecurity became an issue.

Cybersecurity management systems simply inherited the model from what went before. Ring-fencing the cybersecurity management framework and examining it there, will not reveal the problem.

We must first broaden the perspective to look at the business from a distance.

So, in Section One we explore conventional business theories and practices at work, taking a wide view of integrity in business to reveal the true problem.

Section Two offers some solutions, by looking at how it can be done the ESG way, defining Leadership and Social Purpose. We also

introduce and spell out what we see as the 4th Competitive Force –
a major ingredient and therefore incorporated into the book's title.
We also dwell on some very important examples from the world of
business. The consequences of what we see as unethical practices.

Then with Section Three, we narrow the focus on ESG and
cybersecurity. On the way, some readers will pick up valuable new
skills and capabilities that they can apply in other areas of business.
Some readers might be familiar with the theories used to explore
control systems but might find the practical applications demonstrated
herein useful.

You will find in Section Four that we devote our attention to reviewing
the current state of Cybersecurity Management, going on to spell out
the dangers of ignoring the 4th Competitive Force and any lowering
standards in undertaking Cybersecurity measures.

We explore cybersecurity control systems in Section Five, which goes
into the roles people play, including the Board and Senior Executives
and well as those directly engaged in Cybersecurity management.
The role of security consultants is not ignored nor is the importance
of Hard Systems Thinking.

We go soft in Section Six, more specifically with a Soft Systems
Approach, where we look into five different Soft Systems Models.
Scenario Planning comes into play and we look at it in the context of
dealing with a global pandemic and whether it's possible to prepare
for such impactful eventualities.

We propose a New Doctrine in Cybersecurity Management and make
an obvious comparison: ESG versus Conventional Businesses.

In Section Seven we bring things to a head. By Rewiring Business
for Good, we recommend strategies and spell out proposed new
doctrines for business.

Besides offering strategic goals for business, we set out ten steps towards responding, resolving and recovering from cybersecurity breaches, drawing attention to the importance of Threat Intelligence.

Through all this, we expect readers might start to see their businesses from a completely new perspective. If that happens, then this book will have achieved one key objective. Persevere to the end as it will be worth it.

Through our experience and through the examples we provide here, we must stress that most people behave well most of the time. Just some people – just sometimes - will spoil it for the rest by doing things that are wicked, nasty and downright evil.

This then necessitates the creation of a system of justice to deal with bad behaviour. Justice systems are based on moral rules codified in laws, which are enforced through punishment and sanctions of various kinds. Rules are therefore both inevitable and necessary to deal with the few miscreants. To suggest otherwise is to paint a picture of utopia.

However, when it comes to how society has organised the business world, for some peculiar reason it seems to be assumed that there will be no wicked, nasty and evil behaviour: good behaviour is assumed, taken for granted.

The principles of business are not natural phenomena like the laws of physics; they were constructed and developed by earlier theorists and even some who claim to be philosophers. Of course, philosophers have every right to have something to say about business and economics.

To understand the main competitive forces in business it is necessary to revisit these theories. The author recognizes that business principles are more nuanced and much more complicated than is outlined here, but the purpose of this enquiry is to reveal the competitive forces in business in their basic and original forms just sufficiently to expose the critical flaw: the omission of ethics and morals in business practices.

My interest here is in the incorporated business - any business that has the legal status of limited liability. Incorporated businesses are distinguished from sole traders and partnerships by the rule that shareholders' liability is limited to their investment interest in the corporation. There is no legal separation between the owner and the manager in a sole trader. As such, the owner can be held directly responsible for the actions of the business. That is not to say that the same forces are not at work in sole trading or partnership businesses because, let's face it, sole traders can commit wicked acts too. However, for the purpose of this paper, *business means corporation*.

If this approach seems harsh to some readers, we feel it is necessary: to go to what some might view as the extreme of behaviour in order to force the issue to the forefront.

When a reader reflects on his or her own business, they might justifiably conclude that they have not fallen into any of these scenarios in the running of their business. The risk is, of course, that it is all too easy to get hooked into some of these problems at some future time, so hopefully, even for the very best business leaders, there are lessons to be learned.

In the course of completing this book in the first few months of 2020, we watched with horror as an all pervasive pandemic enveloped the world, bringing many businesses to their knees and inevitably – in many cases - forcing thousands of businesses large and small into lockdown and an early demise.

Besides the drastic economic and health outcomes for countries and companies the world over, the Covid-19 outbreak has seemingly given a license to the criminal element everywhere to engage in their dastardly deeds with impunity. While backs are turned, cybercrimes are being committed. So much so that Interpol has posted numerous notices, like this:

> "In response to the rapidly changing cybercrime landscape during the COVID-19 pandemic, the global law enforcement and cybersecurity communities have formed an alliance to protect the public.
>
> "Harnessing the expertise of this alliance, INTERPOL has launched a global awareness campaign to keep communities safe from cybercriminals seeking to exploit the outbreak to steal data, commit online fraud or simply disrupt the virtual world.
>
> "The key message of the campaign, which focuses on alerting the public to the key cyberthreats linked to the coronavirus pandemic, is to #WashYourCyberHands to promote good cyber hygiene."
>
> *Interpol*[3]

Which all goes to point out that every business – large or small – must have a cybersecurity system in place to deal with all risks and eventualities, including cybercrime during health, economic or climate emergencies.

And it also reinforces my strong belief that the best management system to have in place is one that incorporates the principles of ESG management, so that it is ethically, economically, socially and environmentally sound.

SECTION ONE

CONVENTIONS IN BUSINESS

Capitalism is the astounding belief that the most wickedest of men will do the most wickedest of things for the greater good of everyone.

-John Maynard Keynes

CHAPTER 1

The Principles of Conventional Business

Business management practices have developed over time. New management theories have been brought into the boardroom regularly, sometimes following significant events such as the Wall Street crash in 1929, the Enron scandal in 2001, the financial crash in 2008, and so on. In many cases, the lessons learned from these events have improved business. However, it is often forgotten that the ideas of individual people and the theories of business management academics also find their way into the boardroom.

Over time, the origins of these ideas are forgotten, and yet the methodologies and methods derived from these theories continue to be applied without critical consideration even if they cause awful decisions to be made, as they often do. Moreover, the theories transition into doctrines that remain unquestioned and attract a certain reverence. This enquiry will outline some of these theories and their origins to show how business strategy decision-making has been shaped by their methodologies and methods.

There are three important theories that bear down on business. All three embrace the idea of competition.

1) The Free Market Theory

Adam Smith, considered the father of economics, was the first philosopher to be recognised as an author of business theories and economics. These days, Smith's considerable body of work is condensed into a key concept: the free market principle. The core idea is that a market should be about free competition whereby price is determined by a balance between supply and demand, free from government intervention, and free from coercion. It has been widely adopted and forms the basis for trade inside a market and across international boundaries in the global economy.

Hence, the first principle of business is the assumption that the business competes in a free market whereby individuals act in their own self-interest: the free-market theory.

2) The Productivity Theory

The second major development in business management was Taylor's introduction of the reductionist method into management in his 1911 book Scientific Management[4]. His theory can be summarised thus: View the business as a system, reduce it to its functions, reduce each function to its processes, reduce each process to its tasks. Examine where productivity improvements can be made and then make changes at task level to increase productivity. Complete the process by reconstructing the business from the tasks performed into processes and reassemble the functions. This is much like one would engineer a mechanical or electrical system using applied science and is sometimes called efficiency theory.

For Taylor, it was for management to reduce and rebuild, and for the labour force to execute the tasks defined by management. Early business schools, eager to find something to teach future managers, wholeheartedly embraced Taylorism, as it became known. Taylorism revolutionised business management and is still applied somewhat mercilessly by businesses today.

Thus, the second organising principle of business is to improve productivity through the application of Taylor's reductionist method: the productivity theory.

3) The Shareholder Theory

The third principle of business for consideration was introduced by Friedman[5] in his writings on shareholder theory: that the only ethical responsibility of management is to its shareholders. As such, the goal of management is to maximise shareholder value. In summary, the sole purpose of a business is to make a profit: the profit theory.

CHAPTER 2

The Competitive Forces in a Conventional Business

Having identified and laid out the three principle theories open for enquiry, let's now contemplate the business from the perspective of business leaders. Business leaders are operating guided by these theories and their methodologies and methods that have developed over time. The business leaders' decisions are moderated only by their personal ethics and morals or, as Friedman suggested, the laws and ethical customs of society. Hence business leaders apply the three theories of business and make decisions using the three competitive forces as follows:

1. Compete for investment capital by delivering the highest growth in shareholder value and dividends. Investors are constantly looking for opportunities to invest at lowest risk in high yield businesses. This is the profit theory in action.

2. Compete for market share either through offering the lowest price for products and services, or by creating a unique selling proposition to offer differentiated products or services at a higher price. This is the free market theory in action.

3. Compete for the lowest costs (for labour, raw materials, administration, etc.). Driving down the cost of running the business either increases its profits or lowers the price of its

products for increased market share. This is the productivity theory in action.

To emphasise, the only ethical responsibility in the execution of the business is that of the business leader's duty to their shareholders.

Let's now demonstrate the implications of the omission of ethics in business by applying Systems Dynamics using increasingly complex causal feedback loop diagrams.

Systems Dynamics in Conventional Businesses

Systems Dynamics[81] is a powerful tool for revealing the stability (or lack thereof) of control systems used to moderate a business, and for making visible unintended consequences of current business models that are guided only by the three theories outlined above.

Systems Dynamics diagrams comprise of feedback loops showing cycles of cause and effect. At their simplest, these loops may be balancing or reinforcing. Balancing feedback loops are those in which the cycles counter a change in the control systems with a push in the opposite direction. The harder the push, the harder the pushback and so they are stable systems.

Conversely, a reinforcing loop is a cycle of cause and effect in which an action produces a result which drives more of the same action, thus resulting in growth or decline. Reinforcing loops are often hidden and a consequence of factors not considered in the original design of the control system.

Whereas balancing loops seem to provide reasonable control, reinforcing loops, when triggered, drive systems to undesirable and unintended states often at accelerating rates.

Over time, academics and researchers of Systems Dynamics have identified several persistent control systems at work. These have been compiled into a set of standard Archetypes[6], which are used here to reveal the forces at work in some businesses. The analysis introduces the reader to Systems Dynamics with a relatively simple balanced causal feedback loop and then adds more control elements as the enquiry develops. In reading the diagrams consider that a plus(+) feeding into a component has an inclination to amplify that component. A minus(-) feeding into a component has an inclination to attenuate that component.

The Balanced Causal Feedback Loop

Figure 1 depicts a basic control system where the business sets high standards of ethics and morals and responds robustly and instantly to any problem symptoms.

This is intuitively true. It is expected that a business will amplify its standards of ethics and morals as soon as problem symptoms appear and that the raised standards of ethics and morals will instantly attenuate these symptoms. Problem symptoms may take many forms, including:

- Unsafe working practices
- Products that harm the environment
- Products that harm consumers
- Unethical employment practices
- Fraudulent accounting

It is possible to imagine a system where the high standards of ethics and morals is near perfect enough to counter any production of symptoms, but this is unlikely for several reasons. Businesses must often make difficult choices between two equally unpleasant options and in many cases, decisions taken today reveal unpleasant and unintended consequences much later. Nonetheless, in the scenario in Figure 1, the higher the standard of ethics and morals, the fewer symptoms are produced, and if symptoms do appear the business autonomously raises its standard of ethics and morals. The control system is complete, robust and sits entirely within the business.

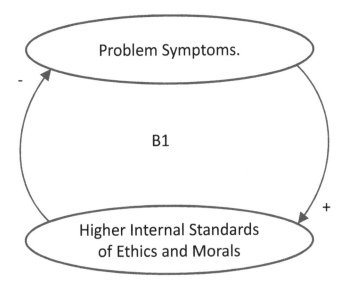

Figure 1   Balanced Feedback Loop

The Perceived Balanced Causal Feedback Loop

People need to feel that global technology platforms answer to someone, so regulation should hold companies accountable when they make mistakes.

Mark Zuckerberg CEO Facebook

Consider however, Friedman's shareholder theory that the only responsibility of business managers is to maximise shareholder value. This shifts the responsibility for ethics and morals to society and lawmakers. Figure 2 depicts a balanced causal feedback loop that demonstrates a control system for businesses where responsibility for standards of ethics and morals lies with government and regulators, and not solely within the business. At first glance, it also seems like a robust control system with opposing forces in balance.

In viewing the systems diagram in Figure 2, the reader must keep in mind that it is not possible to create a perfect control system so symptoms *will* bubble to the surface over time. The higher the standards of ethics and morals the less likely it is that symptoms will appear, and when symptoms do appear the quicker and more effective the response from the business and from the regulator.

In this control system there are two balancing loops at work, B1 and B2:

1) A failure in ethical and moral standards produces symptoms.
2) The business recognises the symptoms and amplifies the standards of ethics and morals.
3) Additionally, the government responds with regulation that forces the business to address the symptoms. (It is also possible that the regulator responds to symptoms produced by another business in the same industry.)
4) This regulation forces the business to amplify its standards of ethics and morals.

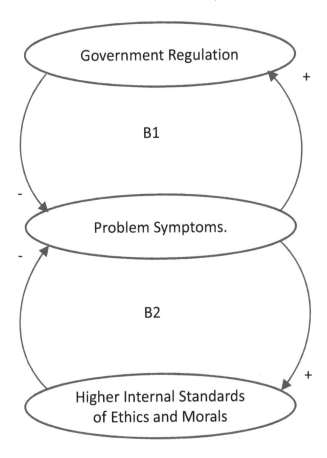

Figure 2   Transfer of responsibility

In short, it is expected that the business will self-regulate by raising its standards in ethics and morals in response to the symptoms it generates, and/or that the regulator will respond to the symptoms generated by the failures in ethics and morals, and act to correct the behaviour of the business.

However, there are three assumptions at work in this balanced causal feedback loop: that symptoms are instantly recognised; that the business and government can respond instantly to address the symptoms; and that the business will instantly raise its internal standards of ethics and morals. But these assumptions are wrong, and in fact none of these actions can occur instantaneously.

Moreover, Norbert Wiener[7] illustrated the difficulty in building a robust control system based on the flow of information between humans, as exhibited in his study of systems that govern through information (cybernetics). Control information is subject to cognitive biases, language differences and cultural differences, to name but a few. Unlike machine-based control systems which have the potential to be very precise, human control systems rely on communications through information which is often unreliable and inconsistent. Hence, the response of the control system will be equally unreliable and inconsistent.

The inevitable delays, plus inconsistent and unreliable human responses will trigger a hitherto unseen reinforcing feedback loop in this control system, meaning that rather than cancelling each other out the forces multiply and spiral, producing even more problem symptoms.

The Hidden Reinforcing Feedback Loop

The lack of synchronicity between the appearance of symptoms, the ability of the regulator to respond with new regulation, and then for the business to raise its standards, triggers a hidden reinforcing feedback loop - see Figure 3. This unintended reinforcing happens because of delays in balancing loop B1 (the regulator) responding to symptoms produced by the lower standards in ethics and morals in the business, B2.

The two balancing loops seem to work as in Figure 2, but once the system accounts for the inevitable delays, the reinforcing loop becomes apparent.

1. d2 and d4 are the delays in problem symptoms appearing and being recognized as such.
2. d1 is the time it takes for governments and regulators to codify new laws and regulations to deal with the symptoms.
3. d3 is the time it takes for the business to enact the higher standards of ethics and morals dictated by the regulator.
4. In the meantime, more symptoms are produced.
5. Having triggered the reinforcing loop, the cycle repeats and escalates.

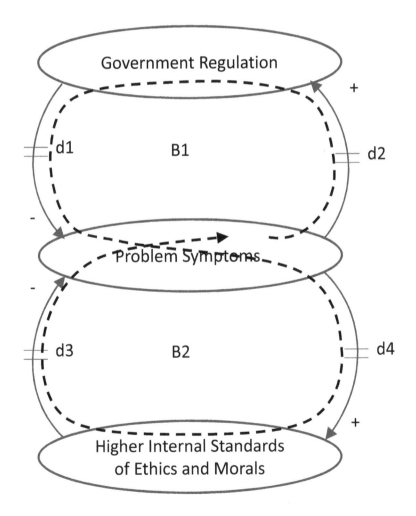

Figure 3 Hidden Reinforcing Feedback Loop

There are many key factors that cause the delays, d1-d4:

- Symptoms might only appear after some time and might be specific to a single business.
- Governments typically codify laws that deal with symptoms rather than the cause which, at its core, is low standards in ethics and morals in business.
- Governments may also be reluctant to encode laws and regulation as it makes the local marketplace less competitive than those of other nation states.
- Businesses are reticent about laws and regulations as they drive up costs. Business often resort to political lobbying to persuade government to roll back regulation. This kind of lobbying may be accompanied by political party donations, all of which makes regulation a political hot potato.

Consider that maintaining a high standard of ethics and morals costs the business money. Hence high standards of ethics and morals collide head-on with the productivity principle that seeks to reduce costs to the business. So, it is inevitable that this collision will cause failings in ethics and morals and will produce problem symptoms.

To demonstrate just how powerful this reinforcing feedback loop is, let's consider two businesses in a competitive situation.

CHAPTER 3

The 4th Competitive Force

Imagine two businesses (business A and business B) that are in competition in the same market for the same clients where their two products are largely indistinguishable. Further, imagine the market has settled into a dynamic equilibrium where product prices are the same and the market share is divided roughly equally between the two competitors. The only distinguishing factor between these two competitors is the standard of ethics and morals of the leadership.

Standards of ethics and morals varies between individuals and, one of the competitors, the one with the lower standard of ethics and morals, revisits his/her organisation and applies Taylor's productivity principle. In the application of Taylorism, the competitor with the lower personal standards of ethics and morals discovers a way to reduce production costs, knowing that the product or production method presents a safety hazard for its employees and/or consumers.

The business leader judges that it is a risk worth taking to gain an advantage over the competitor. In fact, the business leader might even feel compelled to comply with Friedman's doctrine in order to gain a clear advantage for its shareholders. As such, the competitor reduces the cost of their product which earns them a competitive advantage over the competitor with the higher standards in ethics and morals, thereby disrupting the dynamic equilibrium in the market. The company increases its market share and consequently its profits, enabling the business to compete more effectively for investment.

The competitor with the higher standard of ethics and morals now has no choice but to lower the standard of ethics and morals of its business, perhaps even taking a higher risk to regain or achieve the upper hand in the marketplace. The pattern repeats itself in the form of a hidden competitive force. Thus, the previously unseen **4th Competitive Force** is an unavoidable consequence of the combination of the free-market principle, the productivity principle and the profit principle compelling a race to the bottom in morals and ethics. It is a critical flaw in the way the three principles combine to work together.

The Escalation Causal Feedback Loop Archetype used in Figure 4 demonstrates the power of the 4th Competitive Force in a competitive market. When viewing this feedback loop, it is worth keeping in mind that the competitive forces at work in business have a tendency to drive the internal awareness of threats to the business. Leadership periodically perform Strengths, Weaknesses, Opportunities and Threats analysis of the business. The process drives a certain desire to know what the competition is up to through competitor intelligence gathering. Hence, left to its own devices the internal perception of competitive threats to a business will have a tendency to ramp up, creating a form of corporate existential angst which generates a desire to seek advantage over competition.

On the surface, it looks like some kind of dynamic equilibrium is in place between two balancing loops: B1 and B2. However, there is actually a hidden reinforcing loop, shown in red, that flows like this:

1) Business A gains an advantage through lowering standards of ethics and morals, enabling it to manufacture its products at a lower cost, which reduces the price to the consumer, and thus increases its market share.

2. Business A's advantage is a threat to Business B.

3. Business B lowers its standards of ethics and morals and consequently, the price of its products.

4. Business B gains market share undermining Business A's advantage.

5. Undermining Business A's advantage reduces the attenuation on threats to A's business, which is experienced as increased threat, thus corporate existential angst increases and motivates further action.

6. Business A further lowers it standards of ethics and morals, further reducing the cost of manufacturing its products.

7. Business A increases its market share and consequently its advantage over business B.

8. The reinforcing cycle repeats itself and triggers a race to the bottom of ethics and morals.

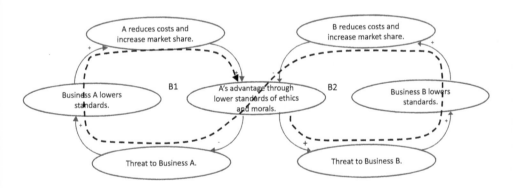

Figure 4   Escalation Causal Feedback Loop

Clearly, there are many good business leaders who maintain the highest standard of ethics and morals, but these standards are not protected in any way from wicked business leaders, nor are they enshrined in law or regulation in real-time. More importantly, they have been specifically omitted from the control system. Hence, the 4ᵗʰ Competitive Force in business - competition for the lowest standards in ethics and morals - will inevitably overcome any intrinsic resistance that good business leaders might have. The desire to survive and compete for investment will ultimately force good leaders to abandon a higher standard of ethics and morals.

Ethical Questions

How can we know for sure that there is a hidden 4th Competitive Force? The hidden 4th Competitive Force in business reveals itself in the symptoms it produces and there are many examples to choose from. These symptoms are produced in the full knowledge of the business leadership, representing a conscious choice to put profit ahead of integrity. Here are a few examples:

1) Knowingly going to market with an unsafe product, e.g. the Ford Motor company with the introduction of the Ford Pinto[8].
2) Knowingly over-promoting Opioid-based painkillers, and in fact denying that they are addictive, which has destroyed communities and hundreds of thousands of lives[9].
3) Knowingly promoting and selling tobacco products to consumers despite awareness of the implications for health.
4) Knowingly dumping toxic waste into rivers and the environment for the purpose of saving the cost of safe disposal.
5) Knowingly enforce zero-hour contracts complying with minimum wage regulation, circumventing laws, thus keeping captive the skills and capabilities of employees, but only paying for them when required by the business[10].
6) Knowingly continuing to use fossil fuels for energy production, even though it is clear the world faces a climate emergency caused by carbon emissions.
7) Knowingly promoting the unsustainable production of palm oil even when it destroys the habitat of one of our most endangered and closely related species, the Orangutan.

8) Knowingly continuing the manufacture and use of single-use plastics even though it has had catastrophic effects on other species and the environment.

These are the kinds of symptoms produced by the 4ᵗʰ Competitive Force, the hidden force at work in business; when left unaddressed it will drive standards down. The only question that remains is: How low can business go in setting standards of ethics and morals?

On a side note, the 4ᵗʰ Competitive Force motivates businesses to compete at the minimum margins of short-term profitability and they cannot cope with Black Swan[11] events. The economic impact of Covid-19 in 2020 and the fallout in bankruptcies demonstrates the fragility brought on by the 4ᵗʰ Competitive Force.

Shifting the Burden Problem

It is of course naïve to expect business leaders to act at the highest standards of ethics and morals, but it is also equally naïve to think business leaders, or at least some business leaders, will not tend towards the lowest standards of ethics and morals. Driven by a desire for the lowest costs and highest profits to please shareholders, even good leaders will lower standards if that brings a competitive advantage.

So, the pursuit of profit in any possible way as long as it is not illegal, has had an unintended consequence - a race to the bottom in standards of ethics and morals driven by the 4ᵗʰ Competitive Force. It takes only one wicked business leader to trigger the hidden reinforcing feedback loop. This is a consequence of Friedman's shareholder theory[12] which has shifted the burden of ethics and morals to the government and lawmakers.

Hence good business leaders and society depend on lawmakers to protect them from wicked business leaders, but in this process, good business leaders are relieved of their personal duty to set the standard of behaviour of their business, and often abandon their personal higher standards to operate at the edge of laws and regulations. Such is the power and pervasiveness of the 4th Competitive Force.

Crucially, the current control framework for business is based on principles that combine to create a critical flaw, the 4th Competitive Force. This, together with business leaders' expectations that the government will regulate the markets, has another unintended consequence. Shifting the burden for setting standards of ethics and morals to government promotes an addiction to regulatory and compliance requirements and to government intervention. See Figure 5.

In this System Dynamics Archetype, the reinforcing loop shown in the dashed line (the 4th Competitive Force) increases business dependence on government intervention through regulation and compliance requirements:

1) Lower standards in ethics and morals produces symptoms.
2) The government increases regulation which directly addresses the symptoms.
3) Businesses increasingly operate to comply with standards set by regulators, thus the business's dependence on government regulation is amplified.
4) Increasing dependence on government regulation attenuates the internal standard of ethics and morals to the minimum level determined by the government.
5) Lowering internal standards of ethics and morals produces more and different symptoms.
6) Increasing symptoms prompts the government to increase regulation to address the new symptoms.

7) The cycle repeats, promoting a dependence on regulatory and compliance requirements, often with a growing time lag and increasingly severe symptoms.

Delays at each step are compounded: delays in the symptoms appearing, the time it takes for governments to regulate (especially with all the political ramifications that go along with regulation), and for the business to respond. Multinationals and global businesses see the problem amplified by the differences in regulation in the different countries in which they operate.

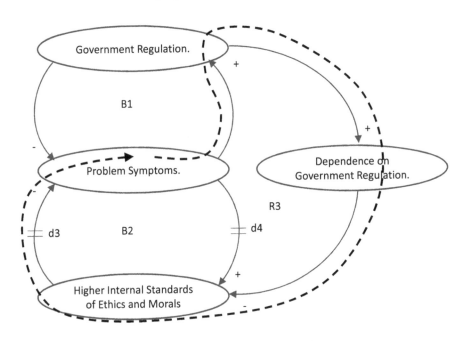

Figure 5   Dependence on Regulation

Next, with increasing regulatory and compliance requirements enforced through sanctions, businesses face increasing risk from regulatory fines, risk of litigation (class action lawsuits), and compensation to clients accompanied by expensive legal costs. Additionally, the leadership team might be exposed to criminal charges and face prison.

Developing an Addiction to Risk Management

After Friedman's shareholder theory[13] was published in the 1970s, business leaders increasingly adopted the profit principle through the 1970s and 1980s, and made decisions for the benefit of the shareholders, often at a cost to society. The profit-at-any-cost principle was further reified by Jensen and Meckling in their 1976 paper Theory of the Firm[14], also known as the agent theory, in which they argue that business managers are agents for investors.

Governments responded to increasing ethical and moral shortcomings brought about by the 4th Competitive Force by codifying and enacting regulatory and compliance laws and, by necessity, enforcing these through fines, restricted market access and even criminal sanctions. In the 1990s, businesses increasingly had new regulatory and compliance risks[15] to face and, on advice from business consultants, invented a compliance and risk management function.

The introduction of the risk management and compliance function was accompanied by the appearance of the risk control framework: a collection of policies, practices and standards that were inserted into businesses. The risk management and compliance function required authority to enforce standards of ethics and morals which they drew from two places: firstly, the regulator conferred the authority to enforce what needed to be done to comply with the laws; secondly, the board of directors consented to enforce a risk management framework from a standards organisation, such as National Institute for Standards in Technology (NIST) or the International Standards Organisation (ISO). The risk management and compliance function also necessitated the creation of the internal audit function, a team to check that the operational units were performing in compliance with the agreed standards.

Overwhelmingly, control frameworks dictate the distribution of duties through Responsible, Accountable, Consulted and Informed (RACI) matrices, which has the tendency to centralise and shift the burden of control to the risk management and compliance team. Figure 6 demonstrates the effects of this, using the Addiction Archetype.

To recap, the risk management and compliance function develops a dependence on laws, regulations, and risk management frameworks to perform its duties, and to enforce these it assumes the authority of the regulator and the board of directors. Consequently, the control system generates a growing addiction in the risk management and compliance function to external intervention which is demonstrated by the reinforcing feedback loop imposed on the business. The Addiction Archetype control system in Figure 6 reveals the hidden feedback loop that amplifies the addiction:

1) The 4ᵗʰ Competitive Force lowers the standards of ethics and morals which produces problem symptoms.
2) The government increases regulation to address the symptoms. Regulation is accompanied by fines and sanctions for non-compliance, which presents a financial risk to the business.
3) The business now requires a risk management and compliance function, to act as an internal regulator assuming the authority of the government regulator with the permission of the board.
4) The risk management and compliance function increasingly depends on regulation to control the business as without regulation it has no authority. Increasing dependence on intervention and heavier legislation necessitates an increase in the headcount of the risk management and compliance function and its associated costs.
5) In tandem with additional regulation comes the risk of fines and sanctions which provides further justification for increasing the headcount of the risk management and compliance function, also driving up its associated costs.
6) Shifting the burden of setting standards in ethics and morals to the regulator, and control to the risk management and

compliance function, lowers the internal standards of ethics and morals to the level demanded by the regulator.

7) Because of lower internal standards in ethics and morals, new symptoms appear prompting the government to increase regulation and concurrent risk of fines and sanctions.

8) The cycle repeats, growing the dependence on regulatory and compliance requirements with its accompanied risk, which increases the cost for managing risk and compliance.

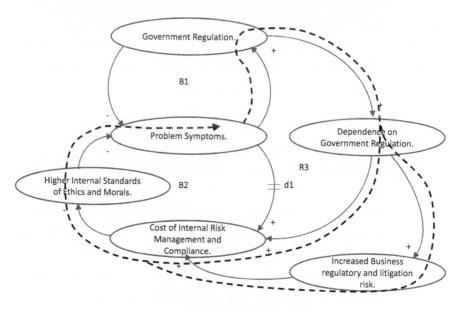

Figure 6   Addiction to Regulation

In summary, the 4th Competitive Force drives the business to operate at the edge of the law, bending the rules rather than breaking them. This creates risk for the business in the form of litigation risk (particularly in the USA) and risk of compliance and regulatory fines (more likely in the EU). Hence, the logical consequence of the 4th Competitive Force is that it ultimately generates risk for the business.

Left to its own devices, business will pursue profits at the lowest cost moderated only by the codified ethics and morals imposed by governments because of old-fashioned ideas about how a competitive edge is achieved. Business leaders are not compelled or encouraged to apply their own higher standards of ethics and morals and they have been omitted from the control system.

Standards of ethics and morals compete against lower production and labour costs, higher prices for products and services, potential loss of competitiveness in the marketplace, and consequently loss of market share. Inevitably, lower returns are followed by the loss of investors. Consequently, ethics and morals were expelled from the boardroom. The primacy of the profit principle, intense competition for lower costs and higher sales, profit margins and investment capital will drive ethics and morals to the bottom of what the law allows.

Addiction to risk permeates the business and leadership increasingly take a short-term view on profits. They operate the business within the margins of acceptable risk, or within the *risk appetite* of the board. Without exception risk management calculations are anchored in probabilities: the likelihood of success or failure. Big data analytics and more data analysed through Artificial Intelligence and Machine Learning offers promises of a better future.

Leadership takes the view that history repeats itself, that data about the past performance of the economy provides certainty about the future performance. This approach demonstrates an ignorance of the difference between possibility and probability. Possibilities are dismissed as these events are too unlikely and should not influence decision making.

As such, a business that has fallen foul of the 4ᵗʰ Competitive Force prioritises efficiency over efficacy. Businesses will reduce costs to the point where they reduce effectiveness to the point where it meets their risk appetite. They operate within the margins of acceptable risk and has little resilience and cannot deal with *possibilities* or Black Swan events. The Trump administration is a prime example of prioritising efficiency over efficacy business thinking, that Trump considered the possibility of a pandemic too low a probability and significantly cut the budget of the Centre for Disease Control. He claimed "I'm a businessperson. I don't like having thousands of people around when you don't need them," Trump said. "When we need them, we can get them back very quickly."[16] The Covid-19 pandemic rolled across the world only a few months later. The United States government was unprepared, and its response was dismal, delayed, and catastrophic for its own people. What Trump failed to realise is that some events are possible and their likelihood unpredictable as to when they will occur, and that ineffective is, by definition, inefficient.

Running businesses and economies on the principle of maximised risk driven by the 4th Competitive Force creates a fragile system that is all too easily upended. All it takes is for the regulator to fall asleep at the wheel or worse still, to abandon his post altogether. It gives rise to a nasty form of economic management which George Manbiot calls disaster capitalism[17]. As an example, he sites mega industrial farming in the USA that produces chickens so infected with bacteria and pathogens that the carcasses need to be washed in deep chlorine to make them suitable for human consumption. The process isn't perfect, and some 48,000 Americans fall ill every year and 3,000 die. But their lives seem to be an acceptable trade for profit.

Absurdly, the unseen 4th Competitive Force also increases the cost of risk management and compliance. Just reflect on this for a minute. The business is trying to save costs by reducing the standards of ethics and morals. This creates risk for the business which requires a control system - the risk management function. This drives up cost for the business. The control function then forces the business to spend money on ethics and morals. So, what has the business achieved but higher costs for no added benefit?

McKinsey and Company predicts that regulatory and compliance functions will only continue to grow, and so will continue to drive up costs for business, particularly in the financial industry[18]. This view is supported by English and Hammond in their survey presented in the Cost of Compliance report 2017[19].

As previously outlined, the cost to business in compliance and risk management is relatively new, emerging only in the 1990s. Ironically, this cost is brought about by an obsession with reducing costs in line with the 4th Competitive Force, and so is of the business's own making. So how can this be reversed?

CHAPTER 4

What Went Wrong with Conventional Business?

All of the above shows either there is something inherently wrong or there is some misunderstanding in the three principles of business (free market principle, productivity principle and the profit principle) and the way they combine, that gives rise to the 4th Competitive Force. Let's critically reconsider the three principle theories of business.

Smith's free market doctrine: Smith, through observation of markets, saw that price *is* determined by a balance between supply and demand, and promptly declared that is how it *ought* to be, free from government intervention and free from coercion, where individuals act in their own self-interest. Whereas Smith[20] is often credited with the title of philosopher, this approach does not meet philosophical standards. Hume would certainly have been furious with him for ignoring the 'is-ought' problem, that one should not argue from how things are to how things ought to be.

The phrase 'free from coercion' hints at an expectation for people to behave ethically and morally in the free market, but having excluded the government from interfering, it begs the question, who is going to police the market to make sure it is 'free from coercion'? To ensure a market is free from coercion requires regulation. Smith has created a theory that by design contains an untenable contradiction which should at the very minimum raise serious concerns. If governments interfere, as they do with regulatory and compliance laws, then it is a rules-based market which contravenes Smith's assertion that the free market must be free from government intervention.

Moreover, there will always be wicked, nasty and evil people who will do things that require government intervention. What is inescapable is that there is no such thing as a free market and business leaders must accept that their activities will be scrutinized by the society and governments. In fact, the best way for business to avoid legislation and regulation is not to give cause for government intervention. Perhaps this is what Smith intended when saying that markets free from coercion will also be free from intervention and this is unrealistic.

Thus, it is inevitable that all markets are rules-based and it is a misnomer to refer to free markets. This is also true for so-called free trade agreements. 'Free trade' agreements are, in fact, conditional trade agreements subject to a set of rules, which controls either the harmonisation of regulation or the application of tariffs where harmonisation cannot be agreed. These rules often invoke a trade-off between different unrelated products or services. Some industries benefit whilst other lose out. There are always winners and losers.

Smith also stated that individuals always act in their self-interest. This is a claim too far. Whereas individuals sometimes act in their self-interest they also at times act in ways that are altruistic, compassionate, generous, charitable and kind. Furthermore, western societies are more inclined to embrace the idea of the individual and its self-interest whereas eastern societies are more inclined to embrace the idea of community[21].

Hence the principle of self-interest is not universal, but a cultural phenomenon. Such is the adaptability of humans that if a system is created around the principles of individual self-interest then individuals will take on self-interest in order to participate in the system. As such observers of Smith's free market might have thought he was right about self-interest. But eastern societies with a strong sense of community also operate successful free markets. Thus, Smith's claim that self-interest is a fixed principle driving the free market does not stand up to scrutiny.

Taylor's productivity doctrine[22]: Taylor argued that the theories, methodologies and methods used in science and engineering must be brought into business management in order to improve productivity and efficiency. However, science and engineering are based on Aristotle's first principles which were invented as the necessary tools to build 'a body of knowledge' about the natural world. Karl Popper's contribution was the principle of falsifiability. Both Aristotle and Popper emphasised that the domain for the application of scientific methodology and methods was fundamentally *the natural world*. This cannot be stressed enough.

Goldsmith[23] provides a comprehensive, albeit brief description, of what science is. There is no need to repeat his definition in detail, but for this one point: scientific theory, methodology and methods were invented to examine and build a body of knowledge of the natural world.

Business is not a natural phenomenon. Business is a social construct built around theories developed for social collaboration. In the introduction I presented the interpretative view that a business is a theory first and reality follows. The flow is from theory (the business plan) to reality. This is distinct from theories about the natural world. In the process of building an understanding of the natural world the flow is from reality to theory. The natural world does what it does independent of any theories we might develop in trying to build a body of knowledge in our pursuit to understand it. Thus, the natural world comes before the theory. In contrast a business comes after the theory and does what it does because of the theory. Without the theory the business will not exist or do anything at all. It is therefore ridiculous to treat business as a natural phenomenon that can be redesigned with tools intended to investigate and build knowledge of the natural world. The tools for understanding the natural world will tell you how the business works: it will answer the how question, but it cannot answer the why question. If one wants to know the why question of the business one needs to examine the theory that created it in the first place. One cannot use scientific methods to examine a business at any instant and from that accurately write up the business plan that created it. I propose that this is impossible even over time.

Taylor's idea gifts management a monopoly over talent and grants it the right to treat employees as scientific objects, ready to be enumerated, constrained into performing a set of mundane tasks, denied their talents, and refused their desire to grow. Simply put, this idea is grotesquely unethical, immoral, and inhumane.

Secondly, Taylorism works on the assumption that the market is predictable and stable, which increasingly is no longer the case. Businesses currently face levels of volatility, uncertainty, complexity and ambiguity that have never been seen before. Having centralised control in a top-down command system, a management structure bent on Taylorism is slow to respond to changes in the market that demand (or provide opportunity for) improvements in productivity. Employees at the frontline, who could respond and improve productivity, are prevented from doing so by strictly applied policies, practices and standards under the ever-watchful eye of the internal auditors.

Stewart[24] explored in some detail Taylor's misinformed application of science in business and dismisses the hypothesis with some force. More will be done later to explore the impact of Taylorism in the business.

Friedman's Shareholder doctrine: To recap, Friedman argued that the only ethical responsibility of management is to the shareholders of the business, the owners. In other words, management has a responsibility to increase shareholder value in any way they can. Friedman's use of the concept of *ethical responsibility* is unfortunate in the sense that making a profit for shareholders does not seem to be an ethical problem, rather it is a contractual issue. Nevertheless, the use of the word *only* also suggests that other ethical issues are not the concern of management.

In Friedman's defence, he did suggest that management should make as much profit as possible while conforming to the basic rules of society, embodied in both law and ethical custom.

The relationship between management and the shareholders is a peculiar one. There is a uni-directional flow of ethical responsibility from the management to the shareholders, but no ethical responsibility from the shareholders to management. In fact, legally, shareholders are protected from any liability for the actions of management on their behalf and so could have no compunction regarding low standards of ethics on the part of management. It follows that shareholders could even turn a blind eye if management sold drugs to young children, which of course is illegal and wrong.

The law may very well come down on management, but not on shareholders. Hence, in Friedman's theory there is an asymmetrical and uni-directional power relationship between management and shareholders that hinges on a single ethical factor: to make a profit. Other ethical concerns have been omitted from the power relationship and in doing so Friedman, unwittingly perhaps, transferred responsibility for ethics and morals to society and lawmakers.

The force of Friedman's doctrine was significantly endorsed when he won the Nobel Prize for Economics in 1976. Furthermore, Jensen and Meckling's agent theory gave further significance to shareholder theory. Both theories are based on a flawed idea that has resulted in - and in some businesses continues to justify - awful, unethical and immoral business decisions.

In fact, Agent Theory[25] by design places ethics and morals with the governments and regulators, hence freeing the business leaders to pursue profit by any means that they can claim to be legal. Legally relieved of any moral responsibility, it will be no surprise if shareholders then demand that management conduct themselves in a way in their professional lives that they wouldn't in their personal lives.

In both theories, agent and shareholder, assume or imply that the business is owned by the shareholders. It is conceivable that this understanding worked the other way around, that if the only ethical responsibility of management is to the shareholders then the shareholders must own the business. Whichever way this worked, it has become a widely held view that a business is owned by its shareholders.

This view is challenged by Bower and Paine in their paper Managing for the Long Term[26]. Bower and Paine claims that the axiom that shareholders own businesses is at best legally confusing and at worst simply incorrect. They point out that shareholders have limited liability, limited in fact to their shareholding, which is fewer rights than what would normally be considered the rights and responsibilities of ownership. Shareholders have no right to withdraw their funding from the business, or to use the business's assets to settle their personal debts. Neither can a shareholder claim ownership rights or usage rights over the assets of the business. A shareholder can, of course, transmit ownership of its shares to another investor. They can also in a limited way influence the makeup of the board through a voting system, but they do not have any ownership rights beyond their shares. Nonetheless, the idea remains pervasive in business, that management act as agents for the shareholders and that the only ethical responsibility managers have is to the shareholders, who are the owners of the business.

The myth that a business is owned by the shareholders must be busted once and for all. The word incorporation is based on the Latin word for body, *corpus*. So, incorporation means the embodiment of the business, creating *a legal person*. The fundamental reason for incorporation and the *legal person* is to create an entity capable of surviving its leadership, management, employees and critically, its shareholders.

Hence, the business as a *legal person* shares many but cannot claim all the rights and obligations of a natural person. For example, the *legal person* cannot vote or take up public office, and it cannot be punished in the same way for failing to meet its obligations to society; unlike a natural person, it cannot be sent to prison, however it can still be punished for breaking the law. It can be taken to court and sanctioned through fines and can even be denied access to markets. The *legal person* can be sued for compensation in a court of law when it causes harm to consumers of its products, its employees, or the environment.

Shareholders cannot own such a *legal person*, in much the same way that a natural person cannot own another natural person. In 1948, the UK Court of Appeal ruled that shareholders are not, in the eyes of the law, part owners of the company. The argument lingered until 2003, when the House of Lords, in a final ruling on the matter, confirmed in unequivocal terms that shareholders do not own the business[27].

What are the implications for shareholder theory and agent theory? Simply put, this makes a nonsense of both and they must be abandoned by business management. This is precisely what Environment, Social and Governance (ESG) companies do.

SECTION TWO

ENVIRONMENTAL SOCIAL AND GOVERNANCE BUSINESSES

Acting with integrity is the same as acting ethically and morally.

Richard De George

CHAPTER 5

What is an ESG Company?

I t is encouraging to see corporations abandon the Friedman doctrine. In August 2019, corporate members of the Business Roundtable in New York committed to leading their companies for the benefit of all stakeholders, including customers, employees, suppliers and communities as well as shareholders[28]. However, the matter is not as simple to resolve as that.

For decades, Friedman's doctrine offered business leaders and managers a touchstone for making decisions. Every decision in the business pivoted on the question 'How is this going to create shareholder value?'

In the same timeframe, business leaders, business consultants and business schools have developed methodologies and methods anchored in Friedman's doctrine. Methods including 'the business case', 'return on investment', 'cost benefit analysis' and 'maximising expected utility' permeate business and are employed at every level of management to predict the outcome of a given project for shareholder value.

Hence, a simple declaration such as the one made by the Business Roundtable will most likely succumb to the entrenched methodologies and methods. Friedman's doctrine has become part of the business's DNA and will resist change. No surprise then if leaders of these companies open themselves up to accusation of 'talk the talk, but do not walk the walk'.

For there to be a fundamental transformation in business, leaders must also adopt a new doctrine, a new touchstone or anchor around which decisions pivot. Such an anchor is provided if business is considered a *legal person* with rights and obligations similar to those of a natural person. The new doctrine will underpin all decisions in the business to ensure the good behaviour of the *legal person*.

At the heart of ESG companies is the fundamental realisation that the business, as a *legal person*, is a member of society much like a natural person is a member of society. Natural persons have a duty of care towards other natural persons and an obligation to treat them with dignity and respect. Complementary to this, a natural person has a right to expect to be treated with dignity and respect. The similarity between a legal person and a natural person is eloquently expressed by Bowie:

> *Some features we associate with individual integrity* [of a natural person] *are also characteristics of organizational integrity* [in a legal person]. *For example, both individuals and organisations with integrity are steadfast in their commitment and actions in moral principles.*

> Bowie, N.[29]

In linking the characteristics of individual and organisational integrity, and noting that he also considers behaving with integrity the same as behaving with high standards of ethics and morals, Bowie gives us a way to see that the integrity and moral judgments of the *legal person* are as important to society as the moral judgements of a natural person. Further, it paves the way to authenticity for the individuals in employment and precludes any situation in which an employee is expected to behave in their professional life in a way that they would not in their personal life.

Introducing the Trustee Theory of Business Management

A trustee is someone who, whether appointed to settle a will or to manage a trust fund for a juvenile, makes judgements on behalf of someone who cannot make those judgements.

One difference between a *legal person* and a natural person is that a *legal person* does not have the faculty to make judgements. So, the *legal person* depends on natural persons, employees, to provide the faculty for making judgements. This means employees take on the role of trustees of the *legal person*.

It would be wrong to claim that a trustee can make judgements on behalf of natural persons perfectly capable of making judgements. Edmund Burke[30] found this out the hard way when he claimed that members of parliament in the UK are the trustees of their constituents.

Trustees must have the autonomy to make judgements in the best interest of the *legal person* by exercising its rights and taking responsibility for its obligations to society. Hence, everyone employed by the business is a <u>trustee</u> for the *legal person*.

Distributed Leadership

Trustee theory has major implications for the notion of centralised leadership. Statements such as the one by the members of the Business Roundtable[24] that they will lead their businesses for the benefit of all the stakeholders is in danger of claiming a monopoly over leadership for senior management, which is reminiscent of Taylorism in the way that leadership claims a monopoly over talent and was shown to be unethical on page 61. If businesses adopt the trustee theory in which everyone makes judgements on behalf of the *legal person* then the senior leadership must also be prepared to relinquish their monopoly on leadership.

Therefore, trustee theory calls for a system of distributed leadership which extends to every employee a certain maximum level of autonomy to make judgements on behalf of the *legal person*. Precisely how much autonomy is extended must be determined by factors such as clear communication of the social purpose of the business (explored below), plus a requirement and ability to make decisions coherent with this social purpose. Senior management must enable the intrinsic leadership in every employee in order to empower them to make judgements on behalf of the *legal person*. To do this, senior management may want to look at three levels of leadership:

- Personal leadership where trustees examine their own beliefs and values to determine what motivates them, and how to apply that motivational force towards a positive contribution to teams and to the social purpose and long-term goals of the *legal person*.
- Team Leadership where teams are built around diversity and inclusivity. Team leadership that creates a psychologically safe space for individuals to contribute freely, with the result that team dynamics fire up innovation and creativity. Bringing together a diverse group of people enables individual members to question their own belief systems and to expand their worldviews so that judgements are more robustly tested, which enriches the values of the whole team.
- Corporate leadership where senior leaders communicate and manage the social purpose of the business. However, senior leadership will do well to solicit ideas from teams, and also to set up operational teams to explore and experiment with new commercially viable ideas coherent with the social purpose

goals of the business. Corporate leadership requires more formal processes for making judgements and so there will be a need for an understanding and application of ethical theories, both to make judgements and to decide the social purpose of the *legal person*.

In the process of incorporation, the *legal person* is granted rights and obligations like those enjoyed by natural persons as members of society. The trustees of a *legal person* must make decisions, take actions, and steer the business so that its good behaviour can be judged in the same way that society would judge the good behaviour of a natural person. Thus, central to distributed leadership is the idea that every employee is a trustee of the *legal person* and is tasked with executing its rights and taking responsibility for its obligations to society.

Therefore, to execute the *legal person's* rights and to be responsible for its obligation, its trustees must apply ethics and morals in the same way a natural person would to protect the environment, work towards the greater good of society, for the benefit of its employees, its customers and its suppliers.

Defining a Social Purpose

I also want to emphasise strongly the point about economics being a moral science.

John Maynard Keynes

Much has been written on social purpose and it is currently a hot topic in the business world. Not all of what is written stands up to scrutiny, particularly the notion that every business must seek out a unique social purpose. This is not possible. Apparently, it's hard to rid oneself of old habits and it seems that the notion of 'unique selling proposition' (USP) wants to creep into the process for deciding a social purpose. Or perhaps it comes from Taylor's doctrine that extends leadership the power to be creative on social issues. Social problems are already there for all to see, and so no business can claim for itself a unique social purpose. It can simply choose one.

Since social issues are already there and visible to everyone in society, businesses can work together in a form of co-competition (or co-opetition – cooperative competition) to address their chosen social purpose.

For example, during the Covit-19 pandemic, several F1 Teams combined with designers to produce ventilators for the frontline health services. Furthermore, a business may decide to stand up operational units with a specific social purpose, and only for the duration that is required to address that social purpose. Hence business can look for social issue to contribute to the definition of their social purpose, but there is more to this than meets the eye.

Another common misunderstanding is that a social purpose is only about what the business will do for society. This is too narrow a definition of social purpose. Having a social purpose also means being good for suppliers, customers, employees and shareholders. Hence a company with a social purpose looks inwards as well as outwards and judges its behaviour towards all stakeholders. Having a social purpose means that business must consider the ethical and moral dimension of every aspect of its business, a task that will require more than the personal ethical intuition of the corporate leadership.

The challenge is that this is precisely where the void is in non-ESG businesses. The burden of ethics and morals was shifted to the government and as such the only control framework the business currently have is what is dictated in laws, and it has already been demonstrated that it is not enough to simply try to meet the requirements of the law. Moreover, the current control framework has shifted the burden to a risk management team that enforces the law on the operational management teams.

The leadership must commit to a process of developing and managing a social purpose that demands that corporate leadership step into ethical and moral thinking. Such is the complexity of the judgements they will make and the problems they will face that the leadership will flounder if they try to fill this void by solely relying on their personal moral intuitions.

> [...] a consideration of moral theory is basic for a proper understanding of how to treat moral problems and engage in the analysis of perplexing cases in business ethics.
>
> A reason for using theoretical orientation to business ethics preferred by philosophers is to avoid situations in which discussions of moral problems in business is a little more than the exposure to prejudices of persons who do not generalise beyond their own viewpoint. Discussion and reflection on issues of sexual harassment, executive salaries, whistle-blowing, and the like may lack critical distance due to cultural blindness, rash analogy or mere popular opinion.
>
> Brenkert and Beauchamp[31]

To avoid problems with prejudices and cultural blindness the business's decision control process must be built around formal theories of ethics.

Formal theories of ethics must be applied in every decision the corporate leaders make on behalf of the *legal person* which would include areas such as employment, procurement, manufacturing, trading and investment judgements. To stress the point, senior leadership as well as operational leadership must be able to judge the good behaviour of the *legal person* on a consistent basis against formal theories of ethics. A business is a social collaborative effort and is emphatically an exercise in ethics and morals. It cannot be and has never been anything else.

Thus, the trustees at the corporate leadership level of a *legal person* must have the necessary ethical resources available to them to go beyond their personal intuitions in making judgements and deciding the social purpose of the business. Those resources are in established theories of ethics. To give some guidance below is a brief overview of the most important theories corporate leaders must embed in their decision processes and deciding the *legal person's* social purpose and governance standards:

The Virtue Theory or Dispositionalism[32]:

The virtue theory of ethics recognises that it is not possible to define precisely what good behaviour looks like. Hence it is not possible to create a rule that says behave like this or behave like that, in order to be/do good. Take for instance the Golden Rule: 'Treat others as you want to be treated'. On the surface this seems like a sound rule but consider that masochists like to receive pain. If masochists want to be treated this way, then the golden rule will set them free to treat other people the same.

Aristotle[21] recognised that many of the ethical and moral decisions one makes are circumstantial and that the circumstances will vary widely. So, one cannot create a set of rules that will deal with all ethical dilemmas or situations. Rather one endeavours to develop a disposition to always make a decision based on the facts at hand. To do this Aristotle's advice is to always ask three questions:

1) How is what we are doing going to improve the way society works.
2) How is what we are doing going to be good for other people directly impacted by it.
3) Is this a good thing that I am doing.

In short, one has a disposition to always do good.

Teleological Theory or Consequentialism[33]

Bentham and Mill developed an ethical theory that proposes one should consider the consequences of one's actions. From this they derived the principles: do no harm, and, work for the greater good of the greatest number. The decision-maker must always consider the consequences of each decision to determine whether it is for the greater good of the greatest number and whether the consequences of an action would cause harm in any way.

There is a vital role for science here. The sharp instruments of science must be used to discover if there are potentially harmful and unsafe consequences for the users of products and in manufacturing processes. Science has the potential to give early warnings so that corrective measures can be taken to prevent harmful consequences. Furthermore, science has already discovered and brought to the forefront past mistakes in products and manufacturing, that has harmful consequences that demands the urgent attention of business leaders.

The climate crisis brought on by a relentless pursuit of cheap energy, the careless polluting of waterways, and the overuse of chemicals in agriculture causing a degradation in soil, springs to mind. Therefore, applied sciences must be used to address these problems which might be the basis for a social purpose. Once again one can look at how Orbia[34] is using their considerable science and engineering resources to enhance humanity.

The Deontological Theory or Categoricalism[35]

Kant considered Consequentialism to be flawed because it will create scenarios where a trade-off between groups is considered acceptable. It is conceivable that working for the greater good of the greatest number will mean that a small number of people might be worse off. There is no consensus on whether Kant's objection to utilitarianism stands.

Nevertheless, Kant offers business leaders an alternative ethical theory from which is derived the two categorical imperatives: firstly, never use a person as a means to an end, but always also as an end in themselves; secondly, some acts are simply categorically wrong, for example one shall not lie, or one shall not kill another person. Categorical ethics demands that something is wrong to do, or something is right to do, if and only if the rule applies to everyone (universalisation: that the act is either wrong for everyone or right for everyone).

The Care Theory of Ethics[36]

Gilligan's care ethics posits that business has a certain duty or obligation to display empathy towards people. It goes beyond the principle of not causing harm to actively seek out opportunities to help people or communities in need. An example of care theory in action is when a business appeals to the UN sustainability goals to decide the social purpose of a business.

Moreover, the business may look at its own community for social issues that need urgent attention. For instance, in some countries entrepreneurs with a social mindset are developing solutions to provide on demand elderly care services for the local pensioners using mobile apps.

Note that social purpose is the primary purpose of the business and is not the same thing as corporate social responsibility which is a charitable or philanthropic effort.

The Oxford Handbook of Business Ethics[37] and Perspectives on Philosophy of Management and Business Ethics[38] are two must haves in the boardroom library. Both books demonstrate the practical application of the ethical theories surveyed above. It is conceivable that the senior management may from time-to-time solicit the support of philosophers acquainted with the practical application of these ethical theories. The American Philosophical Practitioners Association can help with skilled advisors.

A great deal can be learned by looking at how Orbia reorganised to create seven business units each with a different social purpose[39] based on the UN's sustainable development goals. Like at Orbia, managers will also have to consider how the business behaves in relation to its customers, employees, suppliers, and society, as vital elements of its social purpose.

ESG: Rights and Obligations of the Legal Person

In introducing the notion of the *legal person* on page 62 it was stated that the *legal person* enjoys certain rights and obligations. To explore a greater understanding of these rights and obligations let's look through the lens provided by Honoré: Making Law Bind[40]:

- *Self-ownership*: build on the principle that the *legal person* owns itself and that it is categorically not owned by its shareholders.
- *Ownership rights*: that the *legal person* owns its own assets.
- *Usage rights*: that the *legal person* has the right to use its assets in any way it deems fit.
- *Transmission rights*: that the *legal person* has the right to transmit ownership of its assets.
- *Security rights*: that the *legal person* can demand protection of its assets, its business and that its trustees act on its behalf. Government must provide this protection and that protection must be enforced by the justice system.

Hence the trustees of the *legal person* must execute in such a way as to exercise the rights of the *legal person.*

Secondly, the *legal person* has certain obligations:

- *The duty to prevent harm*: The *legal person* cannot use its assets in a way that causes harm to natural persons or other *legal persons.* The harm principle ties back to Mill's utilitarian theory of ethics.
- *Liability of execution:* The *legal person* is liable for any harm caused in the execution of its business. The *legal person* must therefore be ready to make restitution when it causes harm to employees, customers, and other members of society.

Hence the trustees must take responsibility for the *legal person's* obligation to society, to be a good citizen in the execution of its rights.

CHAPTER 6

Planning for Survival with ESG

ESG and Survivability of the Legal Person

The *legal person* has an interest in its own future - its longevity, survivability and viability - in the same way that natural persons have an interest in their future. Therefore, the trustees of the *legal person* must take an interest in the survivability of the *legal person*. It drives the desire to be profitable, to make best use of the *legal person's* assets and to invest for the long term.

This self-interest will encourage investors to invest and will demonstrate how they will be rewarded for putting their trust in the *legal person*. For an investor's view of ESG companies, see James Chen's ESG Criteria[41]. Trillium Asset Management[42] also provides a condensed but revealing assessment criteria that demonstrates an interest and focus on the long term financial performance of the business alongside environment, human rights, animal welfare, workplace discrimination, product safety and products that can be seen as unethical, as well as transparent corporate governance standards.

The methodologies and methods for ensuring the survivability of the *legal person* are the same as for conventional businesses. But in ESG companies the trustees are securing the survivability anchored in rights and obligations of the *legal person* and coherent with the social purpose they have chosen earlier.

The Process of Strategic Planning

Along with survivability and longevity of the legal person comes the process of strategic planning. In conventional businesses this activity is the sole domain of the board or senior leadership team. This, of course, is incompatible with trustee theory, distributed control, distributed leadership, and mutual accountability. The incompatibility is conceptually intolerable and ought to be enough reason to look for an alternative to conventional strategic planning processes. Furthermore, it is also conventionally flawed giving more reason to abandon some of the methodologies invoked in traditional strategic planning.

The first convention of strategic planning methods is the idea that the future can be predicted by economics prophets. Economic predictions are rarely accurate and are significantly inconsistent amongst these prophets. Economic forecasting is driven by an opportunity for prophets to profiteer from satisfying an uncanny desire for certainty for what is going to happen in the future, a certainty that simply does not exist. Moreover, leadership that built a future for the business based on these predictions are also shaping the future, so inevitably some will claim to have predicted accurately, further driving the irrational desire for more forecasting and predictions. The 4th Competitive Force amplifies efficiency, but as Heffernan says,

> *Efficiency can be lethal; only the extravagant oversupply of creative thinking rises to meet the challenge'*

> Heffernan. M.[42]

The idea that strategy built around certainty based on prediction and forecasting will stand up to the volatility, uncertainty, complexity and ambiguity is no more than wishful thinking and gambling with lady luck.

Secondly, is the notion that history repeats itself. Heffernan[39] dismisses the idea that data collected from the past can be used to predict the future and provide any certainty that the leadership is so addicted to. Contributing to our false sense of comfort from knowing the past is that what we know is already inaccurate and devoid of the context or all - or some - of the factors that shaped that context.

Thus, the past is not a meaningful predictor of the future, despite that popular urban myth that history repeats itself. The power of aesthetic similarity makes us believe that when two things look similar, we assume that they are the same and therefore predict that they will behave the same. Heffernan goes on to say:

> *What we have instead are numerous examples where not only did history fail to repeat itself but believing that it did led to blindness and blunder.*
>
> *Heffernan, M.,*[42]

Pandemic Planning

The Covid-19 pandemic has ruined the 'certainty' of many corporate strategies and saw businesses run cap-in-hand to governments for a rescue. Many businesses that operate under the illusion of tightly controlled margins within a tolerable level of risk and a focus on short term profitability ran out of cash within weeks of the lockdowns being imposed by governments around the world, a lockdown that was essential to protect health services and to save lives.

Yet, some businesses actually prepared for pandemics and consequently demonstrated that they could survive prolonged lockdowns, and even take advantage of new opportunities by focusing on providing support for health care and the transportation of essential goods to vulnerable communities. These businesses prioritise efficacy over efficiency. They pursue effectiveness first and efficiency second. The chief investment officer of a $26 billion fund in Helsinki says the market crisis triggered by Covid-19 has revealed just how resilient ESG assets are[43].

In her excellent book *Unchartered*[44] Heffernan shows that running a business is much like building a cathedral. Building cathedrals took hundreds of years and inevitably the project changed leadership, employees, and investors. Thus, there is an added dimension to the stewardship provided by current trustees of the *legal person*. The added dimension is the responsibility to make judgements on behalf of the *legal person* today, with a view of passing responsibility onto the next generation of trustees of the *legal person*. It follows that the current trustees are also trustees for the future generations that will be employed in the business.

It raises the question on how the temporal leadership of a business performs strategic planning for the long term where there will be periods of uncertainty, volatility, complexity, and ambiguity. The answer according to Heffernan is in scenario planning used by companies such as Royal Dutch Shell to plan for the future of the business in an uncertain world.

Scenario Planning

As with all things business, there are a plethora of thought leaders on the subject of scenario planning. For the purpose of this enquiry let us focus on the Oxford Scenario Planning Process (OSP), the foundations of which Ramirez and Wilkinson explore in their book *Strategic Reframing*[45]. Ramirez and Wilkinson cover a lot of ground, but there are three key ideas that are particularly relevant.

The first is that scenario planning is performed throughout the business, making it compatible with the ideas of distributed control and leadership required for trustee theory, and avoiding the situation where senior leadership colonises the future.

Secondly, participants in a scenario planning exercise are referred to as learners and come from every part of the business, not just the boardroom. Thus, the exercise is built around diversity and inclusivity, creating a safe environment for learners to express their perceptions of the world from their individual viewpoints. Moreover:

> *The scenario planning process enables people critically to assess the mental framework they have been using to perceive their situation; to shift attention to the wider context to enable alternative frames in a safe place.*
>
> *Ramirez and Wilkinson[43]*

Thirdly, referring to learners invoke the notion of knowledge acquisition and generation. Knowledge is about 'truth seeking' and is the fundamental purpose of the scenario planning exercise. Of course, the future has not yet happened, so to claim that one knows the truth about the future is folly, but the future is an emerging story, and much can be done to reveal that emergence. Moreover, scenario planning will quickly resolve ambiguities, as it will test theories of what the future will look like and will eliminate false theories very efficiently.

> *Confidence doesn't derive from force-fitting a determined model but from a quiet belief in human ability to keep asking better questions, to find and build better answers.*
>
> *Heffernan, M.[42]*

There are some facts in the present that will have a bearing on the future, some planned activities that will produce facts in the future and some unknowns for which no facts exist. As such, it is useful to consider the three arrows of time that point at the future[46]:

The White Arrow: The future that is embodied in our action planning.

The Black Arrow: the future that is the momentum of our past activities.

The Shaded Arrow: the future that is coming our way independent of what we are doing or planning.

Thus, the trustees of the business must have the autonomy, control and leadership to participate in developing and managing the strategic direction of the *legal person* which demands that every employee of the business participates in a strategic exercise through scenario planning to some extent. Scenario planning will be explored in more detail later, but for now let's give Heffernan the last word:

> *The emergence of open strategy, in which individuals at all levels can contribute to mapping their organisations future, is much more than a tacit acknowledgement that insight and intelligence exists everywhere.*

> *Heffernan, M.*[42]

CHAPTER 7

ESG and the 4th Competitive Force for Good

Conventional businesses that subscribe to the Friedman doctrine, succumb to the 4th Competitive Force and are driven by competition for the lowest cost and a relentless desire to please investors. Their decision pivots on the profit principle and the productivity principle. In contrast, ESG businesses follow a new doctrine where decisions pivot on the good behaviour of the *legal person*. The ESG business harnesses the 4th Competitive Force by competing for the good of society, its customers, suppliers, employees and shareholders.

It is, at the very least, conceivable that the hidden reinforcing loop revealed in Figure 4 can turn into a positive competition, a race to the top for the highest standards in ethics and morals, and that a higher standard of ethics and morals is advantageous, not only in the market, but also in competition for investment. See Figure 7:

The reinforcing loop shown in the dashed line will turn the 4th Competitive Force into an accelerated force for good in business as follows:

1) Business A has an advantage in that its higher standards of ethics and morals enable it to increase its market share, even though its products might be more expensive.
2) Business A's advantage is a threat to Business B.
3) Business B raises its standards of ethics and morals.
4) Business B gains market share undermining Business A's advantage.
5) Undermining Business A's advantage reduces the attenuation on threats to its business.
6) A rise in threats to Business A amplifies its standards of ethics and morals to regain its market share.
7) Business A increases its market share and consequently its advantage over business B.
8) The cycle repeats itself and there is a race to the top of ethics and morals.

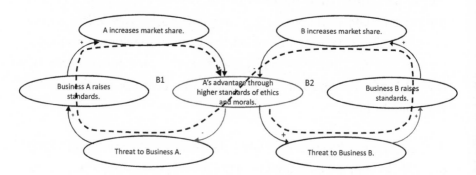

Figure 7   Escalation in Competing for Good

Let's just consider what motivations need to be in place for the businesses to have a positive reinforcing loop for the 4th Competitive Force.

The Will of the Leadership

Leadership must recognise that they are trustees for the *legal person* and know that they are responsible for the rights and obligations of that *legal person*. To simply abandon Friedman's doctrine, although a step in the right direction, is not enough. As such the leadership in an ESG companies must change how the business makes decisions, what its social purpose is. Progress in business leadership is accelerating.

Public Sentiment

There is an increasing public sentiment that motivates and rewards good behaviour in business, driven largely by an increasing awareness of the climate crisis, but also by an increasing personal awareness of social responsibility and engagement. This is particularly relevant amongst the younger generations of consumers and employees. Millennials and generation-Z employees are more likely to leave a business if it has a single-minded focus on making a profit[47]. In contrast, their loyalty increases significantly when businesses are seeking to be a force for good in society, but only if it sits at the heart of the business and permeates throughout.

During the last decade or so, businesses have increasingly funded social projects through Corporate Social Responsibility (CSR) departments and, positive as this might be, it is not the same thing as having a social purpose. In many cases business do social good but continue to subscribe to Friedman's principle. It creates a level of concord in the CSR department, but not in the rest of the business. There is also a worrying trend that some businesses are renaming their CSR departments to ESG departments, but the purpose remains the same.

The Investors

Investors have the potential to be the most powerful force for good. Presently, within the legal framework and the investment community, there is a critical distance between investor motives and standards of ethics and morals. For many investors, the profit motive is simply too powerful.

Nonetheless, there is an increasing number of investment funds that focus on ESG companies. Investors are noticing that they receive better returns from ESG companies in the long term, even when measured using conventional methods.

Investors are also increasingly coming to the realisation that their investments in non-ESG companies are at risk as the survival of these businesses are being questioned. Some investors have declared a clear intention to divest from non-ESG companies within the next decade[48]. Additionally, investors are also becoming more astute in checking the ESG credential of the *legal person*[19].

The Government

Government interference in a free market goes against Smith's principles, but increasingly governments are compelled to intervene in business behaviour through regulation. Encouragingly, a growing body of evidence suggests that regulators are happy to leave ESG companies alone or give them access to markets that would otherwise be restricted[49]. So, there is growing evidence that the best way to roll back regulation is for businesses not to give cause for government intervention in the first place.

CHAPTER 8

Turning the 4th Competitive Force Around

Reversing the trend towards higher risk management and compliance and its associated costs to the business may be simpler than it seems at first. Refer to Figure 8.

The causal feedback loop in Figure 8 turns into a very noteworthy reinforcing loop when business leaders abandon Friedman's doctrine and in its place adopt a new doctrine where they act in the best interest of the good behaviour of the *legal person*. It is not possible to eliminate some of the forces associated with regulation, so they remain in place but increasingly fades into a shadow of the force previously experienced. There will still be wicked people that will produce symptoms and government will respond with regulation after all. Consequently, the direction of flow of the forces remain the same, but keep in mind that the strength of that flow is reduced in ESG companies:

1) Higher internal standards of ethics and morals produces fewer problem symptoms.
2) Reduced problem symptoms reduce the need for government regulatory intervention.
3) Reduced regulatory intervention reduces the amplification for the business to become dependent on regulatory intervention.

4) Reduced regulatory intervention reduces the amplification of the business risk of litigation and fines.

5) Reducing the risk of litigation and fines further reduces the size of the risk management and compliance teams and thus the cost.

6) The business operates at a higher standard and does not need to be controlled by the risk management and compliance function; thus, it reduces or even eliminates friction between the business units and its internal risk management and compliance function.

Hence, the control system in Figure 8 presents a hypothesis that the business will reduce the cost of risk management and compliance if it pursues the highest standards in ethics and morals in the business operations. This is precisely what ESG companies experience.

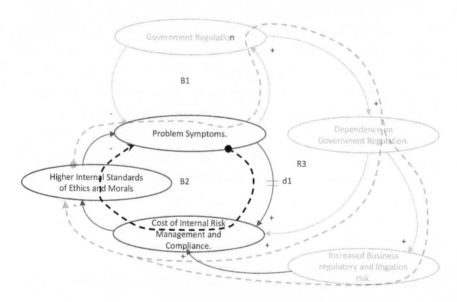

Figure 8   Reducing the addiction to regulation

ESG Framework Creates Value

If this hypothesis is true, there should be examples of businesses that operate at the highest standards of ethics and morals, that investors prefer and that produce higher returns. McKinsey & Company has published research that clearly demonstrates the advantage for businesses that operate with the ESG Framework (See Five Ways That ESG Creates Value[50]). Some notable results from research involving 2,000 companies:

1) ESG companies can take advantage of new markets and increase top line growth.
2) ESG companies benefit from increased sales to socially conscious consumers.
3) ESG companies benefit from reduced costs that increase operating profits by as much as 60%.
4) In case after case, strong ESG companies benefit from reduced regulatory intervention and therefore reduced cost of risk management and compliance.
5) Plus, they are given access to markets and opportunities that would otherwise be restricted.
6) ESG companies benefit from a sense of social purpose in the workplace which brings about an employee productivity uplift that contributes 2.8% to 3.8% higher shareholder value over the long term.
7) A strong ESG proposition increases assets by prioritising investment in long-term sustainable opportunities.

Investors such as Blackrock are increasingly turning to ESG companies for long term positive returns on investments and lower investment risks[51]. Furthermore, the Financial Times reports that Companies with *Strong ESG Scores Outperform, Study Finds*[52]

Something curious seems to happen when one applies the *legal person* principle with its rights and obligations as the principle anchor to decision making. If all the stakeholders take an interest in the good behaviour of the *legal person* as executed by its trustees then all decisions get anchored in a simple self-evident truth, an axiom. With this axiom in place:

- Investors will take an interest in the good behaviour of the *legal person* in their decision to invest. There is a groundswell in investors declaring clear intention to divest from non-ESG companies in favour of ESG Companies[46].
- Procurement departments in ESG companies will take an interest in the ESG standards of the suppliers to the *legal person.*
- Employees will take an interest in the good behaviour of the *legal person* in relations to employment practices.
- Customers will take an interest in the good behaviour of the *legal person* in its ethical marketing and sales practices and pricing.
- The regulator becomes increasingly distant in its intervention of the *legal person* because of its good behaviour.

The conclusion from this is the idea that for a business to work in the best interest of all its stakeholders, all decisions must be anchored in the good behaviour of the *legal person.*

The End of Friedman's Doctrine

In one sense the enquiry has come full circle. Denning[53] described Friedman's doctrine as 'The world's dumbest idea' and the enquiry has exposed the folly and direction has been given where businesses should go. But not enough has been said about conventional business and not enough direction has been given for the viable futureproof business. There is still the matter of Taylor's doctrine and a need to replace it with something new.

To do this the enquiry must narrow down the general concept of ethics and morals. There are different domains in ethics and morals, domains that vary somewhat and, in some cases, require a somewhat different approach. Some of the domains where ethics and morals play out are:

- Product safety
- Health and safety in the workplace
- Corporate corruption
- Corporate fraud
- Unethical commercial practices
- Employee management practices
- Tax avoidance practices
- Environmental harm and the climate crisis
- Ethical leadership
- Cybersecurity

To explore further in all domains in which ethics and morals play out will not only duplicate some effort but will also extend the original purpose of the enquiry. According to the World Economic Forum Global Risk Review[1] cyber risk or cybersecurity and the impact of technology on society are the second most critical risk requiring urgent attention. So, staying true to the title of the book it is right then that this enquiry is concerned with the ethics and morals in the domain of cybersecurity. Therefore, the enquiry will narrow its focus on cybersecurity to undo Taylor's doctrine.

Much have been written about and there is a considerable discourse around the problems of environmental harm and the climate crisis. It is the most critical threat to the future of humanity, and it is right that so much resources are dedicated to address the immediate threat facing humanity and the world. Additionally, at the time this book is being finalised the grim reality of the Covid-19 pandemic is still unfolding. At times it makes the cybersecurity problems seem trivial, but when wicked, nasty and downright evil people try to exploit the Covid-19 tragedy by abusing information systems it stresses the urgent need for society to come to grips with the cybersecurity problem.

SECTION THREE

ESG AND CYBERSECURITY

More and more data about each of us is being generated faster and faster from more and more devices, and we can't keep up. It's a losing game both for individuals and for our legal system.

Cameron F. Kerry[54]

Chapter 9

ESG's Implications for Cybersecurity

Having outlined the framework for the application of higher standards in ethics and morals and the benefits for the business, let's now show that the framework is also applicable specifically to cybersecurity management.

Definitions of Cybersecurity vary from 'Protecting against the unauthorised access of confidential information' to 'The set of controls that maintain the confidentiality, integrity and availability of business data in its various forms'. The problems with these definitions are that they don't drive a distinction between the process of creating information and the process of preserving information, and therefore omits from the management framework considerations on what information is captured and how it is used.

In the introduction we proposed an understanding of cybersecurity as the security of the system that governs through information. This meaning gives a much stronger interpretation of what cybersecurity is, and makes for an urgent call for action.

There is a critical requirement to bring into cybersecurity a process that considers the governance of technology. The World Economic Forum has called on business leaders to take urgent action to put in place mechanisms that will ensure technology is used for good and causes no harm to people[55]. Thus, it will become clear that the scope of cybersecurity must be extended to include governance of technology and how information is used. Let's start with a survey of the ethical and moral dimension of information technology and security in the context of a system governed through information.

Environmental Dimension of Cybersecurity

Blockchain cryptocurrencies like bitcoin already consume more power than Switzerland[56]. Super datacentres for cloud-based computing will consume more power than 20% of the global power generated by 2025[57].

The electronic waste that comes from making, selling, and using, electronic devices for short periods and then discarding them in favour of the latest gismo is a growing concern. eWaste is producing some 50 million tons of toxic material annually and this is expected to grow to 100 million tons by 2050[58].

As such there is a direct link between information technology, its power consumption, the waste produced, and the climate crisis.

The Social Dimension of Cybersecurity

The notion that cyber means to govern through information brings into sharp focus that information plays an increasingly important, maybe even crucial, role in personal, community and national security. Weaponization of information to harm individuals, businesses, communities, and nation states has become a critical threat that affects everyone. The discourse in cybersecurity circles must increasingly include and assessment of what information is captured and how information is used, what it is used for and how it can be weaponized to cause harm to individuals, societies and the business.

As such security *in* information is as critical as securing that information and the *legal person* must consider the social implication of cybersecurity in protecting its rights and be responsible for its obligations.

Capturing the Value the Business Creates

The business as a *legal person* has a duty of care to ensure the integrity, confidentiality and availability of the information that is used to convey the value it creates and to govern the business. The integrity of the information is crucial to the proper governance of the *legal person*, its dealings with suppliers, customers, employees, society, and investors. Those individuals who capture the business value in information have a duty of care (an ethical and moral obligation) to capture the truth in information, so that the information accurately represents the value that is being created.

The consumers of this information (management and decision-makers, tax collectors and investors) have a duty of care towards the *legal person* to make decisions on its behalf, to exercise its rights, and be responsible for its obligations. As such, the consumers of the information that represents the value the business creates gets a certain security from information, a sense of security that the *legal person* is performing in line with their expectations, strategies, and goals.

Creating Value in Information

In some instances, value is created in information rather than capturing value in information. For instance, businesses that focus on product design create value in the design documents. Furthermore, there are instances in every business where decisions are made and documented in minutes of meetings, research documents, and business plans. These documents not only are the value being created, but also captures the value being created in the judgements being made by the trustees of the *legal person*. Trustees of the *legal person* have a duty of care to capture this value accurately, to protect the value and to be responsible for the obligations that the value will not cause harm to the *legal person*, its employees or society.

Preserving the Value Captured in Information

The information system must protect the integrity of the information being captured, must protect the confidentiality of this information, and must maintain the availability of the information for both the creator and the consumer. In the context that cyber is to govern through information this is the ethical responsibility to secure that system. The persons who develop, engineer and maintain the information system have a duty of care towards the *legal person* to ensure that the information system protects the availability, integrity and confidentiality of the information that reflects the value the *legal person* creates.

Governance Dimension of Cybersecurity

> *Ethical questions, too, are overlooked. Where does the data come from, who gave their consent? And who's making money from whom, for what? AI systems already in operation make mistakes, but it is unclear whether responsibility lies with the company deploying the software, the business that design it or the legal system that permits it. These early implementations of AI resemble nothing so much as a drug trial on an unsuspecting public in a market with no oversight.*
>
> *Heffernan, M.*[42]

Governance of technology is a growing concern. There are many ways in which technology can be used in harmful ways but for the purpose of this book let's reflect on social media platforms.

The First Social Media Platform Dilemma

Social Media Platforms provide a means for everyone to express their opinions. The information being captured (the opinions, personal news and life stories, sharing of other stories) does not reflect the value the business generates. As such, there is no duty of care to make sure that the information is truthful or accurate and relevant to the *legal person*. The conditions for protecting the rights and obligations of the *legal person* does not apply here.

Those that work on behalf of the *legal person* that owns the social media platform will meet the rights and obligation of the *legal person* and the users when the platform protects the availability, confidentiality and integrity of whatever the users capture. Having no say over the content being created on the social media platform produces a dilemma for the *legal person* and its trustees. On the one hand the *legal person* must stand up to protect the right of freedom of expression in the use of its platform. On the other hand, freedom of expression is often abused and harmful. The *legal person's* platforms can be used to cause harm to individuals, communities, society in general and to undermine democracies.

The COVID-19 pandemic in early 2020 demonstrated how prolific the abuse of social media platforms can become through the spread of harmful and ineffective health advice, racial, ethnic and religious hate speech to the extent that the United Nations Secretary General Antonio Guterres felt compelled to intervene.

The Second Social Media Platform Dilemma

Social media platforms do more than enable its users to express their opinions. They also capture information that enables the owners of the platform to profile its users. Personal profiles are sold to other businesses and used for micro-targeted advertising to profiled users. At first glance, this seems like a reasonable business model, but the Cambridge Analytica[59] scandal demonstrated that it can be used in sinister ways. Cambridge Analytica sold services to mostly right-leaning political movements to profile social media users and target them with advertising to manipulate elections in favour of Cambridge Analytica's employers. Social Media platforms are also used by foreign governments to interfere in elections in ways that created favourable geopolitical conditions[60] for their countries.

When the *legal person* allows its platforms to be used in this way the trustees of the *legal person* may be in dereliction of their duties to the *legal person* for its obligation not to cause harm to society and individual people.

Artificial Intelligence and Machine Learning

There is much debate around Artificial Intelligence and Machine Learning and how these technologies adopt prejudices. It is possible to deal with this problem by careful screening of the learning data sets[61]. The *legal person* therefore must consider the ethical and moral issues related to the development and use of Artificial Intelligence and Machine Learning.

Extending the Scope of Cybersecurity

In consideration of these ethical dimensions, Cybersecurity must therefore be seen not simply as the task of protecting information assets from unauthorised access, but also should be viewed as an activity that ensures information is used for the greater good of society, that it causes no harm, and that it also benefits the individuals that it serves. The dilemmas posed by social media platforms, artificial intelligence and machine learning necessitates a clear and urgent need for some form of Governance of Technology[62].

The Future of Cybersecurity

In summary, the predicted power consumption of blockchain technologies and super data centres puts it firmly into the 'E' of ESG. Information technology can and is being used to cause harm to society and individuals and is a fundamentally social problem. On the positive side, information technology will play a crucial part in the UN's sustainability development goals where it will be used as a force for good. As such cybersecurity falls firmly into the 'S' of ESG. Governance of technology and asking question about what information is captured, how it is used and who owns it is a critical governance concern, the 'G' of ESG. Furthermore, if we take cyber to mean to govern through information then the security of the information ecosystems is a critical social concern.

It is therefore reasonable to claim that applying the same Systems Dynamics analysis to cybersecurity management in the business will produce the same conclusions. In the first instance it will show that the control system is folly and unnecessary expensive. Furthermore, ESG principles applied to set high standards for cybersecurity in a business as opposed to pursuing compliance with regulatory requirements will cost less.

SECTION FOUR

EXPLORING CYBERSECURITY CONTROL SYSTEMS

Never bring the problem-solving stage into the decision-making stage. Otherwise, you surrender yourself to the problem rather than the solution.

Robert H. Schuller

The difficulty lies not so much in developing new ideas as in escaping the old ones

John Maynard Keynes

CHAPTER 10

Systems Dynamics and Cybersecurity

L et's now reflect on the problem of the standards of cybersecurity using the theories, methodologies and methods used to explore the general concepts of ethics and morals. That is to say, the enquiry applies Systems Dynamics to reveal how conventional businesses manage cybersecurity. It reveals the same shifting the burden problem, the dependence on external intervention problem, and the increasing addictiveness to regulatory requirements. It may feel somewhat repetitious, but there are important distinguishing facts and confirmations that will be considered when exploring how cybersecurity risk management developed over the last three decades or so. The reader should excuse the brevity of the Systems Dynamics discussions, but the risk is either that it is too brief, or it is too repetitive in which case it is better to opt for brevity.

As we narrow our focus on cybersecurity and delve deeper into the business it is necessary to deconstruct the business somewhat. A business is normally divided into departments, functions or operational units such as finance, human resources, procurement, production, sales, customer service and so on. Multinational businesses divide into business units for each country first before they divide into operational units. Of course, every industry will have a different business model and naming convention.

Furthermore, it is a misconception that hackers attack a business, they attack operational units and the systems, data and networks under their control. The enquiry will use the term *operational unit* to mean business unit, business functions, or department. It will soon introduce the risk management and compliance function that controls the cybersecurity standards in the operational units.

Cybersecurity and the Perceived Balanced Feedback Loop

At first, the same perceived balanced causal feedback loop seems to be in place in managing standards of cybersecurity. Things did not necessarily start this way. Cybersecurity may not even have been a serious concern for most businesses and technology companies. The business drive to benefit from ever increasing technological advances saw the development of the internet, more powerful personal computers and wider access to information. Businesses took advantage of this to promote profits in their companies and over time to reduce operational costs by giving its consumers and business partners direct access to their internal systems. Banks exploited this new technology to increase the ease of banking and simultaneously reduce the cost of maintaining extensive branch networks. Online businesses took advantage of online shopping platforms to compete with brick and mortar businesses at much lower costs.

It is only when these businesses started to experience network breaches, the leaking of personal identifiable information, online banking fraud, computer viruses and such, and when it became front page news that regulators intervened. Prior to regulatory intervention some businesses implemented risk management frameworks for cybersecurity as a matter of best practices, not regulatory requirements.

It matters little which came first - best practices or regulatory requirements - as the process for explaining the problem may start at different places but will build up to be the same. Therefore, the enquiry starts with a control system where the regulator intervenes. In that way the burden of cybersecurity was shifted to regulators. See Figure 9.

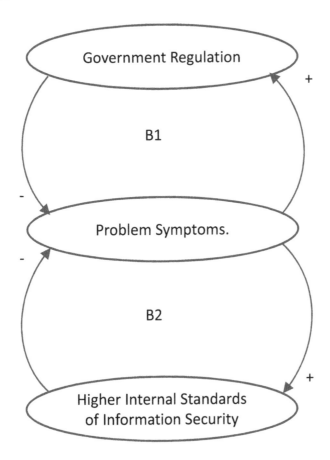

Figure 9 CS and the balanced feedback loop

The perception of the control systems in Figure 9 is that both government and the business strive for higher standard in cybersecurity. However, just as in the case of other business practices that includes an element of ethics and morals the control system works only on the assumption that both business and the government can instantly recognise the symptoms. As symptoms appear, they are addressed instantly by raising the standards of cybersecurity. This is not the case. It took years for regulators to catch up with online fraud, invasion of privacy, computer viruses, etc. and to set minimum standards of cybersecurity. Not all regulators care and, in some industries, regulators to this day provide only limited guidelines and no legally enforceable standards.

Cybersecurity and the Hidden Reinforcing Feedback Loop

The control system in Figure 9 as it is designed has a hidden reinforcing feedback loop that is triggered by delayed and inadequate responses. Refer to Figure 10.

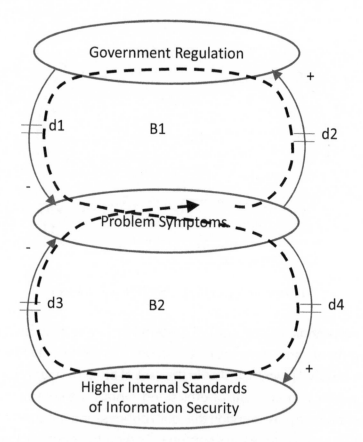

Figure 10   CS and the reinforcing feedback loop

There is an inevitable delay in the symptoms of lower standards in cybersecurity appearing, d2. There is an additional delay in the government responding with regulation to address these symptoms, d1. The business will take time to implement the new regulatory requirements. In the meantime, new symptoms appear which prompts the government to extend the regulatory requirements.

In contrast to other risks, symptoms of lower standards in cybersecurity such as vulnerabilities in systems, applications and networks might linger around unnoticed for many years. They only become visible when hackers exploit the vulnerabilities to gain access to a network.

In the early stages of computer hacking governments tried to deal with the problem by codifying laws such as the computer misuse act that made it a criminal offence. The problem of computer hacking existed for some time before governments enacted laws, but these laws are increasingly difficult to enforce across national borders. Moreover some 15% of computer hacks are perpetrated by government agencies in the 'National Interest'. There is no need to single out any one country, they are all at it.

Additionally, laws on the use of personal identifiable data were created only after it became clear that businesses were abusing this information, selling their consumer contact lists to other business and not protecting personal data. Cyber criminals realised that personal identifiable data can be used for identity theft and then to defraud the individual or other companies by pretending to be that individual. It became increasingly clear that businesses had to spend money on securing their systems and the personal identifiable data of its clients.

Once triggered the reinforcing feedback loop generates a certain dependence on the regulator to set the standards which is fuelled by the 4th Competitive Force.

CHAPTER 11

The 4th Competitive Force Returns to Cybersecurity

Lowering Standards in Cybersecurity

High standards in cybersecurity costs money. As such it drives up costs for the business, reduces shareholder dividend and in a competitive situation will put it into a disadvantaged position against a competitor that spends less on cybersecurity. See Figure 11.

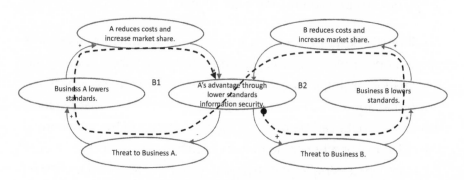

Figure 11   CS and the escalating feedback loop

The hidden reinforcing feedback loop demonstrates that if one business benefits from a cost competitive advantage in lowering standards of cybersecurity then other businesses will follow by lowering their costs by spending less on standards in cybersecurity.

The 4ᵗʰ Competitive Force is the critical force that works against higher standards of cybersecurity.

The corporate existential angst generated by an internal perception of competitive threats to the business generates a desire to seek advantage by doing as little as is necessary on standards of cybersecurity. It generates a certain curiosity in business about how much their competitors are spending with the view to limit its own spending.

There are some tell-tale signs when a business is trapped in this control system. When employing a cybersecurity consulting firm to perform a cybersecurity review or framework gap assessment, the business also wants to know how it compares in standards of cybersecurity with other similar businesses, its competition. Additionally, they ask for a comparison on how much the business spends and how much its competition spends. This kind of business thinks it is considered a valid strategy to be slightly better than its competitors and a desire not to be the lowest hanging fruit, in other words, not to be the most attractive target for cyber criminals or hackers. It mistakenly assumes that all hackers are opportunists that look for the easy targets and ignores the fact that some hackers target specific businesses.

But how low can the standards go? Since both competitors expect the regulator to set the standards, they become increasingly dependent on the regulator to define the standards of cybersecurity. This is a classic characteristic of the shifting the burden problem.

Shifting the Burden to Government

The 4th Competitive Force shifts the burden for higher standards in cybersecurity to the regulator and generates a dependence on government intervention. Driven by a desire to remain cost-competitive, business leaders expect the regulator to standardise the cost of cybersecurity for all businesses under its jurisdiction: to create a level playing field. See Figure 12.

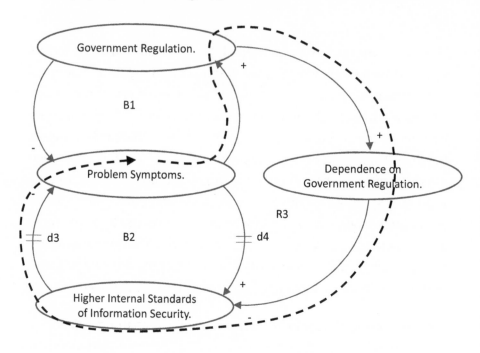

Figure 12   CS and the dependence feedback loop

Businesses see regulatory intervention as setting a standard of spending to which all their competitors must adhere. In Figure 12, competition for the lowest cost impairs the higher standards of cybersecurity. It takes just one business with poor standards in cybersecurity to produce symptoms to trigger regulatory intervention. Having triggered intervention, the regulator imposes standards of cybersecurity to address the symptoms on all businesses under its jurisdiction. Businesses that may have been inclined to set high standards of cybersecurity now have a benchmark set by the regulator and a tendency to reduce internal standards to the level that the regulator demands. Meanwhile, delays in this control system produces more symptoms followed by more regulation. As such it triggers the reinforcing feedback loop in the control system that increases the dependence on government regulation.

The regulatory standards are enforced through fines and other sanctions. For instance, The EU data privacy commission has the right to impose fines of up to 4% of global turnover of a business in cases of serious personal identifiable data breaches. Data breach fines present a considerable financial risk for any business that operates under the EU jurisdiction. To manage the new financial risk, the business inserts a cybersecurity risk management and compliance function.

Developing an Addiction to Risk Management

To perform their duties, the risk management and compliance functions assimilates the authority of the regulator to enforce the standards of cybersecurity required under the law. If this is not enough, and it rarely is, the cybersecurity risk management team persuades the board to implement a control framework from one of the standards organisations such as ISO or NIST. What else can they do?

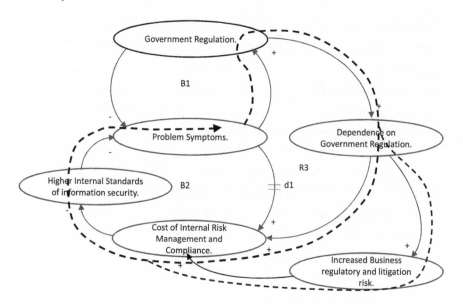

Figure 13   CS and an addiction to regulation

Figure 13 illustrates a reinforcing loop that intensifies the dependence on regulatory and compliance requirements to a point where it becomes addictive. Hence this control system coamplifies a form of addiction to frameworks, laws and regulatory requirements. This addiction is disclosed in the Cost of Compliance Report where one of the survey findings suggest that the continued focus on regulatory risk is unremitting with 70% of firms expecting the cost on managing regulatory risk to increase over the coming year[63].

Addictiveness is particularly heavy in the financial industry. In fact, the financial industry is having to deal with regulatory costs in a way that can only be described as a near out-of-control cost[64]. Granted, banks face compliance risks beyond cybersecurity such as detecting and preventing money laundering and corruption, etc.

Nevertheless, there are some general tell-tale signs that appear that demonstrates businesses have shifted the burden of standards in cybersecurity from the operational units onto the internal risk management and compliance function, triggering an addictive reinforcing feedback loop:

1) The cybersecurity profession is experience a near epidemic of burnout amongst cybersecurity risk professionals[65].

2) Businesses are experiencing high levels of staff turnover with some 42% of cybersecurity professionals predicting they will leave their employer within the first year if they find it has a culture that puts them in conflict with the operational units.

3) Businesses experience difficulty in filling cybersecurity positions. Most businesses take more than six months to fill a cybersecurity role according to research by ISACA[66].

4) Inside business there is an internal resistance from operational unit managers to implement and/or fund security controls. This has been named the *grudge budget effect* whereby the business refuse to fund cybersecurity initiatives. Some 29% of cybersecurity risk manager complain of insufficient budgets.

5) Yet there is persistent production of symptoms of poor cybersecurity standards: reports of breaches or successful cyberattacks abound in the news with one estimated cost of $5tn, by 2024[67] and another even more serious estimate at US$6 trillion[1] by 2021.

Expanded to the industry as whole, the cybersecurity profession is experiencing an exponential growth in the shortage of cybersecurity experts. In 2016, this shortage was estimated to reach 500,000 by 2022, but by 2019, some estimates predict a shortfall of some 4.5 million professionals by the same year[68].

It is interesting to observe that duty of care towards the *legal person*, to exercise its rights and be responsible for its obligations, have been isolated and centralised in the risk and compliance function and away from the operational units. This shifting the burden problem stems from the theories of Friedman, Taylor, Jensen and Meckling. Consequently, the problem is brought about by the conventional approach to risk management introduced in the 1990s which shall be explored further.

SECTION FIVE

THE CURRENT STATE OF CYBERSECURITY MANAGEMENT

Doing the same thing over and over again and expecting different results is the definition of insanity.

We cannot solve our problems with the same thinking we used when we created them.

Albert Einstein

CHAPTER 12

The State of Cybersecurity in Conventional Businesses

Organisations that rely on traditional scientific rationality and continue to manage using classical strategic management methods and hierarchical structures will make things worse rather than better. The world where complex interdependencies between systems gives rise to non-linear (Black Swan) consequences which are impossible to predict.

Nassim Taleb

The state of cybersecurity in the conventional business cannot be laid at the feet of a single function or person. It has come about because of the doctrines adopted by business over the last four or five decades. Let's look at their contribution from the perspective of different roles in the business.

The Role of the Board and Senior Executives.

The board that subscribes to Friedman's doctrine or shareholder theory will make every decision with the interest of the shareholders at the forefront. In respect to cybersecurity the board faces a dilemma.

On the one hand they must approve spending on cybersecurity activities which reduces shareholder value. On the other hand, the board must accept a risk that will impact on the shareholder value, but it is not clear how likely it is that this risk will realise losses. Faced with two equally unpleasant options, the way out of this dilemma is to declare a certain risk appetite that present an opportunity to escape the dilemma. The board goes to a position where they identify those critical information assets that represent a risk beyond the stated risk appetite and agree on the spending required to secure only those assets. The board derives a certain consolation from having balanced spending with acceptable risk. In doing so boards prioritise efficiency over effectiveness.

It must be acknowledged that the awareness of cybersecurity risk has shifted considerable in the right direction in the boardrooms of some enterprises. There are probably several reasons that have elevated the discourse around cybersecurity. The World Economic Forum have had an awareness campaign for some years now. Moreover, there has been some significant breaches that demonstrated the harm to shareholder value. Furthermore, the propensity of senior executives forced to resign their positions following a cybersecurity incident which inevitably followed by intervention from the governments and regulators provides an incentive for senior execs to take an interest.

In many businesses the senior executives are fully on board with raising the standards of cybersecurity, but this initiative does not seem to settle into middle and lower management. The reason for this can be found in how the business is organised for cybersecurity.

The Role of Cybersecurity Management

Businesses that have fallen victim to the shifting the burden problem have become addicted to cybersecurity management frameworks and compliance standards to manage the risk.

Taylor's doctrine has invaded this space. Cybersecurity professionals derive their expertise from studying and being certified in implementing cybersecurity frameworks. Frameworks take the cybersecurity system and breaks it down into domains, and then for each domain, divides into functions and then processes and task. This is what cybersecurity professionals bring to the table and apply inside a business, and they must have something to bring to the table.

Symptoms continue to appear which demand new policies, practices and standards. To be able to deal with more complex frameworks the risk management and compliance function expands commensurately, requiring more cybersecurity professionals, or demands more from the cybersecurity professionals already in place. Furthermore, Taylor's doctrine encourages the development of increasingly specialised roles where each require combinations of skills and capabilities that are hard to find in one person creating a significant headache for hiring managers.

The 4th Competitive Force amplifies the compliance approach to cybersecurity and motivates operational managers to spend less than their competition in order to guarantee that the cost of cybersecurity is the lowest possible. But bizarrely this approach increases costs in risk management and compliance functions which in turn enforces spending in the operational units. The absurdity of this leaves one speechless.

Furthermore, driven by the board's demand to balance the cost of cybersecurity with the board's risk appetite forces the cybersecurity management function to apply the recommended second step of frameworks. Reduce the scope to include only the critical information assets of the business. This leaves the business fundamentally exposed in other areas. Once again, we see prioritisation of efficiency over effectiveness.

Moreover, risk management and compliance functions assimilate the board's authority to enforce security standards in the operational units through policies, practices and standards. Internal security audit teams periodically assess and enforce compliance to make sure the operational units comply. It exacerbates the internal friction between risk management and compliance functions, and the operational managers.

Risk and compliance management have devised artificial methods and standards to monetise and enumerate the risk through process such as business impact analysis. These risk management frameworks have been designed to build convincing business cases for investments in cybersecurity. It is in an ill-fated attempt to account for the predicted cost of a security incidents multiplied by the likelihood of an attack.

The aspiration that it can be presented to hardnosed senior executives as a justification for spending more on cybersecurity is misplaced. These arguments rarely stack up because there are peppered with conditional statements: 'If we experience this kind of attack it will cost the business so much'. Doing a business impact analysis on a subset of critical business assets is outright subjective; subjective to the people doing the impact analysis and subjective to the business. Such is the subjective nature of this process that no accounting standard can be agreed. Inevitably, the business is compelled to make an objective decision based on subjective information. They are, simply put, costly exercises that rarely satisfies the board.

If all that fails then the risk management team resorts to injecting fear, uncertainty and doubt by drawing analysis from the costly consequences of some posterchild hacks and related data breaches. These are often incommensurate with the business the risk management teams work for.

Analogies are dangerous because they fail to take into account both the differences between events and open exposure to accidents and contingency. No two events are ever exactly the same and not just because of changes over time. Countries are different, personalities are different and everyone operating in the present is different to those from the past.

Macmillan, M.[42]

Thus, these analogies fail to convince the board too. In the end the board is reticent to approve budgets for cybersecurity spending.

The Role of the Subject Matter Expert

SMEs find themselves working in operational roles rather than advisory roles. They often find themselves in a cantankerous standoff with operational managers who are at best disinterested and at worst careless. SMEs are held accountable and must deal with increasing pressure from central control who dislikes the underperformance of the security control. It accentuates the burnout epidemic amongst cybersecurity professionals[45].

Furthermore, SMEs find their skills and capabilities very quickly become redundant. Rapid technology changes in the operational units means they are no longer required. Having been horseshoed into a narrowly defined role to capture their talents they are denied the opportunity to satisfy their desire to grow. All too soon they leave to go to companies that appreciates their skills and capabilities and fire up their desire to grow. The cybersecurity skills shortage in the financial industry is a significant challenge[69] and has resulted in a recruitment war with other industries.

The Role of Operational Management

One way to illustrate the friction between cybersecurity risk management and operational management is to look at those businesses where there is a significant drive for digitisation. Operational units are developing new digital products at pace. The vulnerability manager in the cybersecurity team insists that the new products are penetration tested before they go live. The vulnerability manager has the authority, sanctioned by the board, to decide to go or no-go. In a classic shifting the burden problem the vulnerability manager is accountable for vulnerability management, and the operation unit is responsible to remediate vulnerabilities.

Operational management sees penetration testing as a source of frustration. It slows the project down, drives the cost up and inevitably requires additional resources to remediate vulnerabilities. The developers in the operational unit shifts the burden for security to the penetration testers and the vulnerability managers. One only needs to look at the OWASP[70] top 10 list of vulnerabilities to realise it has not changed much in the last 10 years. Developers are making the same mistakes they did decades ago. So instead of learning how not to make security mistakes in coding, developers shift the burden to the vulnerability manager to test their code to identify mistakes so they can be remediated.

The Role of the Security Consultancies

If Taylor was right then one would expect his scientific approach always to produce the same or at least very similar objective frameworks, but in fact, cybersecurity management frameworks differ substantially which fuels the accusation they are derived at subjectively. This is a consequence of applying theories, methodologies and methods designed for examining the natural world against something that is not a natural phenomenon.

Cybersecurity consultancies exploit the addiction to frameworks and regulatory requirements by offering cybersecurity framework gap assessments followed by remediation programs.

Consultants identify gaps with the framework, identify missing or underperforming controls and then propose a remediation program which is executed in an old-fashioned linear way: the project/programme management approach. Entropy sets in almost immediately as the business progress through the linear approach and time passes. Consequently, the stages deemed to be completed has already become obsolete before the subsequent stages have been started. Things that drive entropy include:

- In pursuit of new business opportunities, the operational units, striving for efficiency, changes or introduces new technology, develops new go to market solutions and in the process undoes the security controls already in place.
- Cybersecurity frameworks change regularly so standards change which means the remediation programme is out of date almost immediately it starts.
- Security controls often conflict with other security controls. The consequence is that some planned controls become redundant or existing controls are rendered ineffective.
- Subject Matter Experts leave the business and therefore the standard slips which is only discovered when the Security Audits reveal lapsed security controls.
- Technology reaches the end of its life, is replaced, and consequently investments in security controls related to the old technology is lost.
- New vulnerabilities are discovered which immediately render the programme out of date.

Having lost control of the programme, the consultancies encourages the business to reset by repeating the gap assessment. The new gap assessment produces a new remediation programme which is also executed in a linear fashion. Entropy sets in again and the business is forced to repeat the process a year later.

There is an expectation in the linear approach that risk will be reduced over time in a somewhat progressive fashion. See Figure 14.

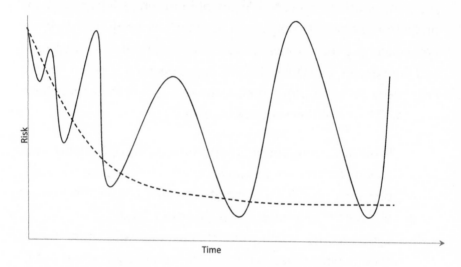

Figure 14   The expected risk reduction

In Figure 14 the dashed line is what is normally promised to the business as the risk management and compliance team executes the linear remediation programme to reduce the risk. The solid line depicts what is probably happening as entropy sets in. Consequently, the security programme is ineffective, and spending is inefficient.

CHAPTER 13

Hard Systems Thinking

Hard systems thinking is modelled around Taylor's idea that it is up to management to design the roles, tasks, skills and capabilities of employees. Most people will be familiar with Hard systems models such as Organisational Architecture, Operational Research, Systems Analysis, Enterprise Resource Planning and Systems Engineering, each of which is significantly aligned with Taylorism.

Cybersecurity managers that appeal to risk management frameworks such as ISO 27K, NIST 800-53 and COBIT 5 are building hard systems to control cybersecurity standards.

At the heart of these frameworks is the distribution of responsibility, accountability, consulted and informed, the RACI matrix. It is worth mentioning that the RACI matrix was introduced into project management in the 1984 paper Goal Directed Project Management[71]. To be fare claims have been made that it happened earlier, but no reliable references can be found.

It seems that a reasonable claim can be made to suggest that it benefits large scale projects that spans operational units where each have a vested interest in the project's success. But for some inexplicable reason RACI found its way into Organisational Architecture later in the

1980s. Precisely what benefits this brings organisational structure and its related processes is not clear, but the damage it does certainly is.

In Hard Systems thinking responsibility and accountability are assigned to two different roles in the business and thus the business is built around a top-down centralised command and control model often with a form of matrix management. Employee roles within the hard systems are assigned operational responsibility for executing hard defined tasks. Management take on accountability for the work done by employees. This idea assumes that the business operates in a stable environment. This assumption may have been valid some decades ago, but increasingly businesses operate in a volatile, uncertain, complex, and ambiguous world.

The hard system of centralised control cannot deal with the variety of challenges the environment throws at it and consequently it breaks down. Some readers might see the irony that centralised control in communist governments were derided, but it is the norm in conventional business management.

Let's consider just what kind of challenges the cybersecurity risk manager faces. In ISACA's *State of Enterprise Risk Management Report*[72] respondents revealed the following:

1) 64% finds it challenging to deal with changes and advancements in technology. Presumably this has something to do with the drive towards digitisation because operational managers are facing a challenging marketplace and being agile has become a business necessity.
2) 42% indicated they find it difficult to keep up with the changes in threats faced by the operational units. The kind of innovation and attack techniques deployed by attackers leaves the cyber defence teams behind.
3) 45% indicated they are finding it difficult to keep up with new threats to the business. In the last few years ransomware

attacks combined with advanced attack techniques have become ubiquitous.

4) 29% indicated that keeping up with legal and regulatory change is challenging. Regulators increasingly must intervene as new symptoms appear.

On the other side of this coin survey respondents revealed:

1) 39% complained of a lack of budget to run an effective cybersecurity system.
2) 52% complained about not having enough cybersecurity professionals in the team.
3) 51% complained about having missing skills in the cybersecurity team.
4) 29% complained about a lack of policies in key cybersecurity areas.
5) 24% complained about a lack of executive support for cybersecurity.

These factors illustrate how a hard systems model is broken by the sheer variety of challenges faced by the cybersecurity and operational management teams.

Ashby's[73] "Law" of Requisite Variety stated that for a system to be stable, the number of states that its control mechanism is capable of attaining (its variety) must be greater than or equal to the number of states in the system being controlled. Hard systems shaped around top-down command and control will always fail to control an environment that throws too much variety at it.

Let's consider this in a systems dynamics diagram. See Figure 15.

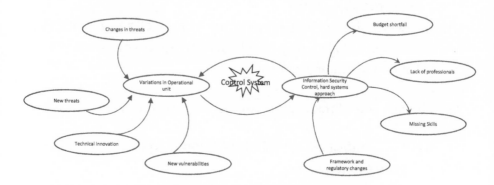

Figure 15   Variety Defeats Hard Systems

The consequence of the hard systems centralised top-down command and control model is that it breaks down in face of the variety and complexity of the cybersecurity problem in the operational unit. Hard systems fail when trying to address an environment that is volatile, uncertain, complex and ambiguous.

The most important criticism of hard systems thinking is that it has a tendency to draw a fence around the business when used to design the cybersecurity organisation: Step 1, Define the Scope. It then considers it as a standalone system operating in a controlled predictable environment. Reality is very different.

The business is fundamentally connected into the environment and the control of that system must be designed so that it can respond effectively to all the variety that the environment will throw at it. It is precisely the hard systems thinking that is exploited by cyber criminals. They can adapt their tactics, techniques and procedures in unexpected and rapid ways to overcome the centralised control system.

Furthermore, in a hard system model, managers claim a monopoly over deciding how the system will respond and employees who are in the frontline of defence execute set tasks that cannot cope with the challenges they face.

Businesses that want to survive in a volatile, uncertain, complex and ambiguous world must not only abandon Friedman's Doctrine but also Taylor's Doctrine. If this is not done urgently, then the business will head for a tipping point where control is lost completely.

CHAPTER 14

Heading for the Tipping Point

Whilst the risk management team attempts to take control of the cybersecurity problem the operational units must continue their business development programme of digitisation and the collection, transmission and processing of data.

As previously discussed, governments are inevitably (and perhaps unavoidably) slow to respond by expanding regulatory and compliance rules. This creates a scenario where eventually the unrestrained and ungoverned use of information technology will reach a tipping point causing significant harm to the business, society and individuals. See Figure 16.

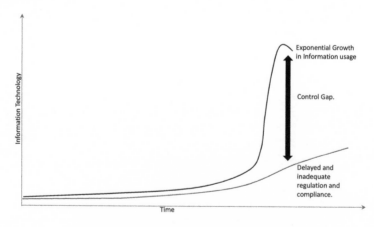

Figure 16   The expanding control gap

The World Economic Forum survey[74] on the global risks considers cybersecurity risk as second only to the climate emergency. As businesses increasingly compete through digitisation and where regulators simply fail to keep up with digital innovation and the use, misuse and abuse of information, the control gap increases. Ultimately the control gap stretches to reach a tipping point where control is lost completely resulting in a significant collapse of the information ecosystem. Polgreen claims that:

'We see it play out every day with the viral spread of misinformation, widening news deserts and the proliferation of fake news. This collapse has much in common with the environmental collapse of the planet that we're only now beginning to grasp, and its consequences for life as we know it are shaping up to be just as profound'[75].

Examples of early signals of the tipping point include:

1) The weaponization of the internet and the use of malware by governments to cause harm to the critical infrastructures of other governments.
2) The stockpiling of undisclosed vulnerabilities by government agencies 'in the national interest' and vendors that offer red-teaming services, which leaves individuals, businesses and society exposed to cyberattacks.
3) The cyberattacks perpetrated by some nation states that target physical infrastructures of other nation states through the internet (Stuxnet[76] on Iranian uranium enrichment facilities and the attack on the Ukrainian power grid[77]).
4) The spreading of misinformation via social media platforms by political activists and some nation states against other nation states, undermining trust in fair elections and democratic processes.
5) Daily reports of data breaches that exposed hundreds of millions of people's personal identifiable information[78].

Striving to operate at the bare minimum of compliance and regulatory standards mean that some businesses operate with standards of cybersecurity below the regulatory control line. As the control gap stretches businesses are increasingly at risk of losing control over the collection of and use of information for profit.

Urgent action is needed. To emphasize businesses must abandon not only Friedman's Doctrine, but also Taylor's Doctrine. For this the business can turn to Soft Systems Thinking.

SECTION SIX

A SOFT SYSTEMS APPROACH

If a system is to be able to deal successfully with the diversity of challenges that its environment produces, then it needs to have a repertoire of responses which is (at least) as nuanced as the problems thrown up by the environment. So, a viable system is one that can handle the variability of its environment. Only variety can absorb variety.

W. Ross Ashby

CHAPTER 15

Soft Systems Thinking and Cybersecurity

A successful organisational system must redistribute control to where it will be most effective in dealing with the variety of challenges. It must extend to the controller a certain autonomy to decide the most appropriate response as long as it is consistent with the overall cybersecurity goals of the business. Compare for a minute the requirement of distributed control and the trustee theory that implements distributed leadership. Crucial to the success of a transformed business based on trustee theory is the dismantling of Taylor's doctrine. This is what soft systems thinking offers organisational design. A business can choose from several soft systems thinking models.

Firstly, the Vanguard[79] method (a systems approach for process complexity) works on the principle that the flow of work in an organisation must be geared to what the customer wants. Thus, the Vanguard method takes an outside-in approach, in which the business model is designed to respond to its customer's needs. It seems to work well where the institution operates without competition such as councils, housing boards and other government institutions and has gained considerable traction with governments.

The methodology relies on the *check-plan-do* actions. Check is analysis of how the current systems performs from the customer's perspective. One might consider the customer to be the operational manager and the cybersecurity team the supplier. It might meet the requirement to transfer control to the operational units, but it will present a problem as it will be hard for the operational manager to judge the performance of the cybersecurity team. The idea that there is a customer/supplier relationship at work will not solve the shifting the burden problem. Hence this is not a promising solution.

Secondly, Systems Dynamics[80] (a systems approach for structural complexity) which the reader should now be familiar with as it is used to understand and manipulate the interconnectivity between components in a complex control system. Systems Dynamics is used in the earlier analysis (balancing and reinforcing feedback loops) in this paper to demonstrate the complex interaction between components, and to reveal the hidden reinforcing loops. It is an invaluable system thinking tool to both uncover unintended consequences and to reveal hidden reinforcing feedback loops.

Systems Dynamics can also be used in ways that directly measure the cause and effect of interconnected components. For instance, in Figure 13 *CS and an addiction to regulation*, the symptoms can be measured as the number of exposed vulnerabilities and the number of breaches or data leaks. Increasing dependence can be measured as increasing regulatory requirements or increasing granularity of requirements. Increases in regulatory fines can be tracked historically and finally, the cost of risk management and compliance can be tracked. As such, it can be used as a business dashboard to constantly monitor friction points and reinforcing feedback loops.

A criticism of Systems Dynamics is that one can put anything into the systems diagram. This can be avoided by making sure that all items can be enumerated in some way. Systems Dynamics can be used to design control systems, but it does not offer advice on how to design the organisational structure.

Thirdly, business might consider Socio-Technical Systems[81] (Systems Approaches for Organisational Complexity). Socio-Technical Systems work on the principle of small groups for self-regulation. In this respect it seems to fit the needs of a new system with distributed control and mutual accountability. Indeed, ISACA incorporated Socio-Technical systems in their Business Model for Cybersecurity (BMIS[82]). Socio-Technical systems thinking brings into play the human element (Culture) in the organisational design of a business. It focuses particularly on how humans interact with technology. Step one: consider why change is necessary. Step two identifies the boundaries of the system to be designed and its interface with other systems.

Step two reveals the problem that provokes criticism. Socio-Technical systems thinking fails because it attempts to ringfence the business or part of the business as if it somehow operates in a closed, controllable environment. The criticism was somewhat mediated by a modification to the methodology to Open-Socio-Technical[83] Systems thinking which brought in environmental factors in organisational design and has gained some traction in the business world.

Socio-technical systems puts a heavy emphasis on technology and how humans interact with that technology, perhaps too heavy to help manage the problem of cybersecurity. It will further encourage those that appeal for more analytics, and more science and more technology to address cybersecurity risk.

Fourthly, businesses may want to consider Stafford Beer's Viable Systems Model[84] (Organisational Cybernetics). The Viable Systems Model is a system that fits perfectly around the principles of distributed control and mutual accountability for the rights and obligations of the *legal person*, and to grant as much autonomy as possible to operational units and individual employees. Managers and employees are free to decide what to do but are required to act in a way that is coherent with the overall systemic cohesion of the long-term goals of the *legal person*. Thus, the systems thinking model meets the demand for a new model for cybersecurity risk management, that is to be able to deal with cybersecurity in a volatile, uncertain, complex and ambiguous environment.

The Viable Systems Model also closes the circle on the meaning of cybersecurity as securing the system that governs through information. It invokes the notion that an organisation is a study of a system that governs through information. An organisation is any form of human collaboration so could be a government institution, business, sports club, charity and many more. Within a business there are cybers for different business lines, business units, departments, and functions. From this we can build a view of interconnected cybers that combine to deliver the global information infrastructure. As such every cyber play a vital role in the security of that global information infrastructure and cybersecurity is the protection of that system. In fact the application of the Viable System Model proposed here will create a system governed through information that protects itself against cyberattacks as opposed to a control system that shifts responsibility for the protection of the system to a function separate from the main business units. A cybernetics that is cybersecure against cybercrime and cyberattacks.

Implementing the Viable Systems Model

In the process of implementing the viable systems model the burden of higher standards of cybersecurity is shifted back to the operational managers in a business. To understand how this is done let's consider the components in the viable systems model. See Figure 17.

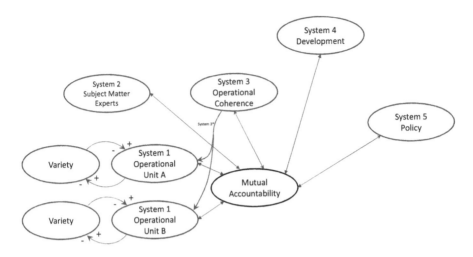

Figure 17   The Viable Systems Model

Figure 17 shows a Systems Dynamics interpretation of a viable system model. At first glance this seems like a complicated control system unlike the robust system first introduced on page 16. But notice the robust balanced feedback loop exist between the operational unit and the variety it will experience in its own area of operations. Also notice that the control signals can vary positively or negatively.

In Figure 17, the business has two operations A and B where each operates in its own section of society and each have to manage the variety thrown at it. An operation here can refer to a business unit or a function of a business unit. The viable systems model will replicate to cater for increasingly complex and layered businesses which divide into business lines, country specific operations etc.

The viable systems model is employed around Ashby's law of requisite variety, that 'only variety can absorb variety'. If a system is to be able to deal successfully with the diversity of challenges that its environment produces, then it needs to have a repertoire of responses which is (at least) as nuanced as the problems thrown up by the environment. At the heart of the system is the notion of mutual accountability (shown in the centre). More will be said about mutual accountability later, but first let's take a closer look at the Control Systems in a Viable Systems Model with a focus on cybersecurity.

System 5: Policy

The senior executive leadership articulates and manages the goals for cybersecurity standards. Consequently, it works very closely with the operational units through the system of mutual accountability to understand their needs, and to set the governance policies that reflect the purpose of the business, the 'why are we here?' question. Operational units must pursue these goals but is allowed a certain maximum autonomy to respond to variety. Governance policies and goals for cybersecurity are set and dynamically managed by the senior leadership team. They must act as trustees for the *legal person* meaning that they have a duty of care to exercise its rights and be responsible for its obligations.

System 4: The Cybersecurity Management

System 4 focuses on what is happening externally and advises the board who manages the long-term goals for cybersecurity standards. It collects information from the operational units as well as monitoring developments in the broader cybersecurity landscape, external to the business. System 4 will maintain awareness of trends in cybersecurity, will assist in the selection of shared cybersecurity technologies such as Identity and Access Management, firewalls, data leakage protection, intrusion detection etc. System 4 has responsibility for recommending cybersecurity technology, but not for the actual deployment or operation of these technologies.

Furthermore, System 4 must have complete purview of the legal and regulatory requirements and must be able to advise the operational units. Finally, System 4 must collect, manage and distribute actionable threat and vulnerability intelligence to the operational units in an accessible and timely manner, through the system of mutual accountability.

System 3: The Cybersecurity Operations

System 3 will maintain cohesion in the standards of cybersecurity amongst operational units and exercises operational control over the cybersecurity technology provisioned to the operational units. Furthermore, it maintains synergy between all the operational units. System 3 has overall day-to-day responsibility for cybersecurity operations, including:

- The security operations centre that monitors and aims to detect intrusions and other security events.
- The recruitment and supply of cybersecurity subject matter experts and advisors to service the operational units.
- Resourcing external consultants and subject matter experts.
- The maintenance of cybersecurity technologies; and advising the business on procuring such technologies.
- The collection of and the distribution of intelligence on new vulnerabilities.
- The collection of and the distribution of actionable threat intelligence.

System 3* serves System 3. System3* is the audit function that ensures the standards of reporting is transparent, accurate and honestly reflects the standards of cybersecurity in the operational units. Furthermore, it verifies that the standards are consistent with the cybersecurity goals set by the board and promulgated by System 2.

System 2: The Cybersecurity Subject Matter Experts

System 2 exists to provide expert consulting and advice in support of the operational units and **not** to be constraining on the operational units. As such, the cybersecurity team will neither police nor enforce security controls. The cybersecurity team is made up of cybersecurity technical experts and advises the operational teams on which controls are relevant and should be implemented around the systems, data and networks. System 2 advises operational units consistent with the goals in standards of cybersecurity set by System 5.

Hence the cybersecurity SMEs support the building of cybersecurity profiles unique to each operational unit. System 2 will use cybersecurity management frameworks as catalogues of controls and will pick those most appropriate to the unique profile of each operational unit. It will be necessary, from time to time, to bring in external subject matter experts to advise the operational units on how to secure new technologies such as when the operational unit moves to cloud and container computing.

Furthermore, the cybersecurity SME is responsible for coordination between the operational teams to ensure that shared security controls work together and that changes for one operational unit will not undermine the standards of another operational unit. Such is the nature of information technology, networks, infrastructure and shared systems that coordination is a critical responsibility of the cybersecurity team.

System 2, like every employee of the business, must work within the principle of being a trustee for the *legal person*, meaning they are responsible for maintaining the rights of the *legal person* and are mutually accountable for failing to meet the *legal person's* obligations. To emphasise, advise from the cybersecurity team must be consistent with the cybersecurity goals of the business.

System 1: Operational Unit Management

System 1 consists of the various parts of the organisation that operates with the maximum allowable level of autonomy consistent with the overriding cybersecurity goals of the business. The way the operational unit engages with the environment brings about unique challenges from a commercial perspective, and also, from a cybersecurity perspective. The level of autonomy extended allows operations to respond to changes within their environments and to make the best of opportunities offered by the unique circumstances of that environment. Hence, management of the operational unit must take full ownership for the standards of cybersecurity of the operational unit under their control.

The Viable Systems Model recognizes that no operational units work in perfect isolation but is connected to other operational units and changes in its environment reflects through to other operational units. Therefore, one operational unit is also fully liable and therefore accountable to other operational units and to the cybersecurity management team for any failings that harm the business or its environment. The key consideration to transferring this responsibility to operational management lies in the fact that the business is a *legal person* with certain rights and obligations. As trustees of the *legal person*, the operational management execute to exercise the rights of the business and take responsibility for its obligations.

For instance, when the operational unit wants to respond to a new opportunity in its environment, it has control of the cybersecurity related to that opportunity. Operational management must decide what security controls are required and what will be in place for the systems, data and networks relevant to the opportunity, but consistent with the overall cybersecurity goals of the business.

In shifting the burden of cybersecurity back to the operational management team of each operation, the business as a whole distributes control where it can be most effective. Additionally, the reporting system is designed around mutual accountability, that is every trustee working for the *legal person* is accountable to every other trustee for the highest standards in cybersecurity. Operational management makes judgements as trustees accountable for their action to execute the rights and obligations of the *legal person*.

Appendix A presents some extracts from ISACA's COBIT 19 and CSF Implementation guide for COBIT 19. Both embraces the Viable Systems Model with distributed control and mutual accountability.

CHAPTER 16

Scenario Planning as a Binding Force

In some quarters of the cybersecurity industry, consultancies and cybersecurity professionals put their senior leadership through cybersecurity event emergency response exercises. Often called Gold Teaming, the board or senior managers are called into an emergency meeting to make critical decisions on an unfolding cyberattack. They are fed partial and ambiguous facts and must make critical decisions under enormous pressure.

There is no doubt about the value of these exercises particularly in securing investment in cybersecurity efforts, but there are deep ethical and moral considerations when the participants are misled to believe that it is a real security event when it is in fact a simulated exercise.

Scenario planning offers an alternative that not only avoids this ethical dilemma - the deception - but balances the objectives of the cybersecurity team with the business drivers of the operational management teams. The purpose of the scenario planning exercise is that of building knowledge within the operational team managers, but also in the cybersecurity team on the business development plan and business strategies of the operational managers. The scenario planning thus fosters the forging of common ground and harmonises the language for describing the future through a process that acknowledges and airs different viewpoints, allowing these to be compared in the 'transitional' safety of the future conceptual space[85].

Moreover, scenario planning eliminates any colonisation of the future by either the risk management and governance team, or the operational management team, but instead blends together the strategic development plans of the operational unit with the requirements for cybersecurity in a coherent manner cohesive with the overall goals of the business.

Target Practice

As a guideline, scenario planners must consider the future from the perspectives of the three arrows of time discussed earlier. Keep in mind that scenario planning participants are referred to as truth seeking learners:

The White Arrow: The future that is embodied in our action planning. The operational management team lays out its business development plans to the scenario planning meeting and solicits input from the cybersecurity subject matter experts (SME) as to what is needed from a cybersecurity perspective. It is important to consider that the cybersecurity and technology governance requirement may render the operational business plans unworkable and as such it requires an open-minded approach from everybody. The white arrow seeks to narrow the control gap shown in *Figure 15 The expanding control gap*, and as such will put some restraint, or even trip a circuit breaker if the operational units expands beyond its own control capabilities.

The Black Arrow: the future that is the momentum of our past activities. The operational management team lays out what they expect to happen in the future based on what they have already done. In the first implementation of this cooperative enquiry the risk management team SME must present the scenario planning team with the security requirements and operational management team must present their compliance and or justification for non-compliance.

The Shaded Arrow: the future that is coming our way independent of what we are doing or planning. The scenario planning exercise must consider what could possibly happen in the future. Here it is crucial to understand the difference between possibility and probability. The consideration must be focused on what is possible and not the probability of the event occurring. There is an unfortunate tendency to look at likelihood times impact in considering risks. Probabilities are relevant only where there is an underlying causal structure that assumes a normal statistical distribution of data collected in the past which is not the case for cyberattacks. Past cyberattacks do not predict future cyberattacks.

Covid-19 has demonstrated what happens if decision making moves from possibility to probability. Nine pandemics have happened in the past one hundred years, but if one calculates the probability of a pandemic over the last one hundred years then the likelihood of a pandemic works out to .09 and most business owners would consider this such a low risk not worth taking into account[86]. Yet, the impact of Covid-19 on societies, governments and business have had catastrophic consequences.

Pertinent to cybersecurity, no one is able to describe a causal connection between the virus that causes Covid-19 and cyberattacks. Yet, the World Health Organisation has seen a fivefold increase in attacks on its systems and infrastructure[87]. Other health care institutions and pharmaceutical companies have not escaped cyberattacks either[88]

> *[…] in VUCA[89] conditions the applicability of probability is limited, so learners would be well advised to avoid seeking accurate predictions in situations where it is illogical to expect these.*
>
> *Ramirez and Wilkinson[90]*

In contrast, possibilities are not calculated based on historical occurrences or frequencies, but always assumed that it will happen. The same is true of cyberattacks. The future (probability of cyberattacks) cannot be determined from the past cyberattacks. The likelihood, is indeterminable. Likelihood of success of a cyberattack can only be determined by two factors, the availability of a vulnerability and if the vulnerability is exposed. Exposed vulnerabilities can be tested for with a reasonable level of accuracy and when vulnerabilities are found they can be fixed or mitigated reasonably quickly. But no one can claim to the ability to read the minds of cyber criminals or state sponsored hackers. Thus, likelihood refers to the likelihood of success based on exposed vulnerabilities and not the motivation of the attacker.

Aristotle and Scenario Planning

Thus, the scenario planners must always consider that a future cyberattack will happen and thoroughly prepare for the event. Information about past cyberattacks (threat intelligence) is valuable in that it is used in cybersecurity scenario planning to test the preparedness of the operational team to respond to a cyberattack and to limit the impact of a successful attack.

When considering the threat of cyberattacks it is useful to take into account Aristotle's perspective on time. Aristotle wrote that time and change is the same thing. If you stop time you will stop change, or if you stop change time comes to a standstill. When analysing a successful cyberattack or data breach it reveals a series of changes that culminates in the successful attack.

From a scenario planning viewpoint, learners should consider the series of changes in the past that will carry through into the future, changes planned that will bring about a new future, and changes coming towards the operational unit that will disrupt its future or provide new opportunities.

Cyber threats are changes that are inevitably coming towards the business and changes made by the operational unit now will build resilience and preparedness to deal with those changes. Thinking about time inevitable injects ambiguity and uncertainty into the decision making process. Thinking of the future as changes fixes that delusion.

Mutual Accountability Reporting and Measurement

Cybersecurity standards must be consistent with the overall cybersecurity goals of the business and must be consistent between different operational units. To facilitate this there is a formal reporting channel shown in the centre in Figure 17, that interconnects all the operational units, cybersecurity management, operations and senior leadership. The formal reporting system conveys information about the standards of cybersecurity achieved by all operational units, and also informs other operational units about changes to environments other than their own and how the affected operational unit responded.

Setting new standards to respond to changes in the environment raises standards of cybersecurity across all operational units. Reporting on standards of cybersecurity goes all the way to operational risk management and the board and in the process of doing so, builds into the system the notion of mutual accountability for cybersecurity standards. The system of mutual accountability builds a 4th Competitive Force for Good into the business, a system where all operational units pursue the highest standards of cybersecurity in a friendly competitive environment.

System 1 must seek advice from System 2 on what questions to ask and what to report. The purpose of the reporting system is to generate in operational units a reasonable level of cybersecurity literacy. It is fundamentally not aimed at building a high level of expertise with operational managers.

That level of expertise is provided by Systems 2, 3, and 4. The reporting system must therefore be simple, clear and sufficiently condensed so that it is easy to generate and to interpret. Hence each operational unit will construct a report on the standards of cybersecurity applied through its unique cybersecurity profiled around its systems, data and networks, but consistent with the overall cybersecurity goals of the business.

This reporting system is designed to foster a security culture which builds five values: transparency, mutual accountability, appropriate systems knowledge, compliance with policies and procedures, and formal communications channels.

Distribution of Decision, Consulted and Informed

Viable Systems Model based organisational design favours the Decision, Consulted and Informed matrix (DCI) over the conventional Responsible, Accountable, Consulted and Informed (RACI) matrix. The RACI matrix runs the risk of centralising control with management and build hard processes for employees. The DCI shifts control back to the operational units and from there to every employee in that unit giving each a level of autonomy to decide what to do relevant to the context in which they have to make a decision:

- **Decision Maker**: Operational management who makes the decision and is accountable for its impact on the business. Decisions must be made with the principle of being a trustee for the *legal person*, to exercise its rights and be responsible for its obligations. Operational management will be held accountable for liabilities caused by bad decisions.

- **Consulted**: Cybersecurity team is accountable for providing guidance based on functional expertise and experience, highlighting issues and raising alternatives to support the Decision Maker.

- **Informed:** Other operational teams, cybersecurity team and risk management committee are notified after the decision has been made and who will need to support the execution of the decision.

A high-level DCI matrix will look something like this:

Activity	Senior Management	Operational Management	Cybersecurity Management	Risk Management Committee	All Operational Units
Strategic goals for cybersecurity	D		C	I	I
Measurement and reporting standards	D		C	I	I
Build Unique Cybersecurity Profiling	I	D	C	I	
Use Operational Units Security Profile	I	D	C	I	I
Build Cybersecurity Team	I	C	D	I	C
Use Cybersecurity Team	I	D	C	I	I
Build Cybersecurity Operations	I	C	D	I	
Use Cybersecurity Operations	I	D	C	I	I
Build Protective Controls	I	C	D	I	I
Use Protective Controls	I	D	C	I	I
Build Detective Controls	I	C	D	I	I
Use Detective Controls	I	D	C	I	I
Build Response Controls	I	C	D	I	I
Use Response Controls	I	D	C	I	I
Build Recover Controls	I	C	D	I	I
Use Recover Controls	I	D	C	I	I

Table 1 Sample DCI Matrix

Not all decisions lie with the operational management. System 5, the board of directors have control over the strategic goals and reporting standards and are kept informed on the standards of cybersecurity in the operational units. Cybersecurity management will make decisions on what security controls and expertise it will provision following consultation with operational management.

The decision to use the security control provisioned by the cybersecurity team lies with operational management. Operational management will be accountable to the board and to the risk committee for the decisions they make. DCI will embed mutual accountability and distributed control into cybersecurity management.

CHAPTER 17

Building Unique Security Profiles

The recommendation is to apply the reporting and measuring standards proposed in NIST CSF[91]. The standard of cybersecurity is condensed into five easy to understand functions.

Additionally, there is an uncanny correlation between the defensive functions in the NIST CSF and the stages in the cyber kill chain. The cyber kill chain was first used by Lockheed Martin[92] following a cyberattack that stole important design documents of their new stealth fighter jet. Over time variations of the kill chain were developed and in the variation below a number of stages have been combined to reduce it from seven to five.

As such the NIST CSF makes visible the preparations that are necessary to deal with the different stages of a sophisticated cyberattack. Moreover, the reporting mechanism can be very easily built into an Excel Spreadsheet. Some examples are available in GitHub[93] and can be easily adapted or customized for different operational units. The NIST CSF framework also provides a handy control reference guide into different frameworks such as COBIT 5, ISO 27K, NIST 800-53, COBIT 2019 and even PCI DSS. The five functions in NIST CSF also denotes a process that must be applied from left to right. Thus, always start from identify and work through protect, detect, respond and recover. Doing the later functions before identify and protect will result in an incoherent and ineffective cybersecurity system.

The NIST CSF proposes a rating system for where a particular control might be performing. The objective is to set tier levels consistent with the critical nature of systems, data and networks. As such it is perfectly acceptable for some systems, data and networks to be at a lower target tier and for other to be set at the highest target tier. Comparison therefore is made between the target tier for a control and the current tier for that control.

The comparison provides a simple measurement system for all the controls in a function. For example, if the target tier is set to two and the current tier the control achieves is set at one, then the control is assessed to fail its target tier. If the target tier and current tier is the same, then the control is assessed to be meet its operational tier. The following table presents an example measurement system.

Tier	Current Tier	Target Tier
One	Not Implemented	Not Required
Two	Implemented for first time or ad-hoc	Required

Three	Established and control is applied consistently	Control is documented and must be well defined and applied consistently
Four	Control is applied consistently and reviewed periodically. A record is maintained of the review process and change control is in place. Minutes of review meetings are recorded	Control is applied consistently and must be reviewed and adjusted periodically in response to changes or business requirements.

The table enables the measurement of both the standards of cybersecurity and whether the operational unit is compliant with its own standards.

The cybersecurity team will advise the operational unit managers on what questions they should ask and be able to answer relevant to their unique security profile. The questions proposed here are compatible with the references one will find in the NIST CSF, but the language have been simplified somewhat to eliminate the technical jargon often present in frameworks.

Operation managers will identify all systems, data and networks under their control and for all of these will apply technology governance with the aim to minimize data.

On Technology Governance:

1) Have you catalogued all the systems, data and networks used and owned by the operational unit?
2) Does the data capture the business value the operation generates for the business? If not, consider removing it.
3) Does the data create value for the business in some other way? If not, consider removing it.

4) Have steps been taken to identify toxic data (such as spreadsheets on individual user computers that contain personal identifiable information (PII)) on the network, data that is not under cybersecurity controls?

5) Have you considered the ownership of the data and if you don't own it, have you removed it?

6) If you must use data owned by someone else have you obtained formal/legal permission to collect, process and store this data?

7) What are the limited usage rights you have obtained for the data owned by someone else?

8) Have you taken the necessary steps to protect and limit access to information owned by someone else?

9) Are you using information in a way that could be harmful to the owner of that information?

10) Have steps been taken to identify vulnerabilities in the systems and networks that capture, store and transmit data?

The shadow of legal and regulatory requirements cannot be avoided and must be taken into consideration when systems, data and networks have been identified to make sure that the operational unit is at minimum compliant.

1) Who in the company is responsible for the legal and regulatory requirements in the countries in which it operates?

2) What are the implications (financial or restrictive) to the business if we do not comply in any one of the countries in which we operate?

3) As we operate in Europe, are we compliant with the requirements for GDPR?

4) Does GDPR requirements apply to countries in which we operate outside of the EU and if so, are these other countries GDPR-compliant?

5) Have we calculated the full financial costs for non-compliance in all the countries we operate and has this been included in the cybersecurity risk assessment?

6) Have all relevant legal and regulatory requirements been taken into consideration for building out our cybersecurity profile of each operational unit.?

7) Have we had an external independent audit performed on our legal and compliance requirements in all countries, and what were the findings?

8) How are we keeping up to date with changes in the legal and regulatory requirements in each of the countries in which we operate?

9) Have we received legal counsel on the legal and regulatory requirements in each of the countries in which we operate?

10) Do we operate in any country where the legal and regulatory requirements bring into question the viability of the business in that country, and if so, should we consider pulling out?

The following are sample questions about what protective controls have been built around the systems, data and networks of the operational units. These questions will be specific to each system, its data and its network and the cybersecurity team will advise the operational units.

1) What physical access controls are in place in corporate offices and branches, and have they been tested for effectiveness?

2) Do physical access controls systems connect into the internal network and have they been tested for vulnerabilities?

3) Is the internal network completely within the physical secure area or are there any access points outside of this, such as WIFI, and has the access points been tested for vulnerabilities or configuration errors?

4) Is the internal network protected with firewall technology and has this been tested for configuration errors and other vulnerabilities?

5) What technology is in place for internal user (employee) identification and access management (IAM)? Has it been tested for secure configuration and vulnerabilities?

6) Does the IAM support granular user role access control and has this been tested for configuration errors and vulnerabilities?

7) For online and mobile applications, how does the user authentication work? Does it have two-factor authentication? Does it allow for role-based access control? Has this been tested for vulnerabilities?

8) Is data encrypted both in transit and at rest? Have the encryption technologies been tested for vulnerabilities and configuration errors?

9) Has the costs and effectiveness of these processes and technologies been reviewed from an investment view and are there any savings to be realized?

These questions relate to what preparations are in place to detect potential cyberattacks on each of the systems, data and networks under the control of the operational unit.

1) Is there an intrusion detection system in place and has it been tested for effectiveness?

2) Are we monitoring logs and events of the systems, data and networks?

3) Have we performed use case analysis to identify correlation rules for the SIEM?

4) Have we tested these correlation rules to see if appropriate alerts are generated?

5) Do we have technology in place to analyse and report on anomalous user behaviour?

6) Do we have technology in place to detect malicious code on the systems and networks?

These questions determine what preparations have been put in place to respond to cyber events and what response plans have been built specific to the systems, data and networks used by the operational unit.

1) Have we identified the threats against the systems, data and networks of the operational unit?
2) Have we prepared playbooks and decision trees in the event of detecting an attack?
3) Have we rehearsed these playbooks?
4) Have we got incident response capability to deal immediately with an attack?
5) Have we got a communications plan in place in the event of an attack on the systems, data and networks of the operational unit?

These questions are to determine the preparations of the operational unit to deal with cases where an attack was successful.

1) Do we have a communications plan in place so that we can inform the relevant external stakeholders (regulators, customers, the press etc.)
2) Have we got a formal process aimed at improving protection, detection, respond and recovery processes in the aftermath of an attack?
3) Have we got business continuity, backup and recovery plans in place in the event of a successful attack?
4) Do these meet the operational unit's service requirement and have they been tested.

To facilitate high standards in cybersecurity and to ensure consistency with the business's cybersecurity goals, the operational units must consult with the cybersecurity team within the business: System 2. Periodically, the security team will augment or propose changes to the questions System 1 must ask and must report on.

Systems 1-3 make up the autonomic management of standards in cybersecurity to make sure that operational units pursue the highest standards consistent with the goals of the business whilst simultaneously having the autonomy and flexibility to respond to changes and opportunities in its environment. Thus, cybersecurity becomes blended into the operational changes and business development goals necessary for the viability of the operational unit, rather than being viewed or experienced as a rigid constraint put on the operational unit. Systems 1-3 focuses on the here and now so that it can respond to the variety of challenges thrown up by the environment it operates in.

Cybersecurity Technology Governance

More needs to be said on the subject of Technology Governance. The EU CANVAS Project examined the deeply seated ethical and moral issues at stake in cybersecurity. As with the CANVASS project businesses can do well to apply the three ethical theories in how it sets standards for cybersecurity.

Businesses that strive for the highest standards in cybersecurity will ask some pertinent questions wherever there is a touchpoint with information. These touchpoints can be online digital systems, internal systems for capturing business value in information, or point of sale terminals. Perhaps in our modern era life is mostly digital, but cybersecurity under the theme of security of systems that govern through information, refers equally to verbal communications and paper communications. Additionally, it applies equally to operational technology and internet of things devices.

Having moved the centre of control to the operational management team it is they that must ask the ethical and moral questions for the systems, data and networks that support their business operation. Furthermore, as every employee act as a trustee for the *legal person* (the business) it is necessary for every employee to have at least a good understanding of their duty of care when they touch information. Sample questions must include:

1) How is this system and the data we capture, store and process improving society?
2) How is this system and the data we capture, store and process improving the lives of people touched by it?
3) In capturing, storing and processing this data, am I being a good person? Am I maintaining the integrity, confidentiality and availability of the value I capture in information for the business?
4) Will this system and data cause harm to any other person or the environment?
5) Will this system and data use a person or persons as a means to an end and not also as an end in themselves?

Every system and data-owner (operational unit manager) must become familiar with Tony Honoré's[94] thoughts on ownership. The importance of Honoré paper cannot be overstressed. It is the foundation of many laws that enshrines ownership rights around the world. He defines nine important 'incidents' of the concept of ownership, which are listed here and made specific to the ownership of information:

1) *Ownership rights*: to have full physical control of information.
2) *Usage rights*: to have full enjoyment of information.
3) *Management rights:* to decide how information will be used.

4) *Income rights:* to derive income from information.

5) *Capital rights:* to have the information destroyed or deleted.

6) The *right to security*: to remain the owner of information indefinitely or to choose to have it destroyed.

7) The *right to transmissibility*: to pass ownership on to another person of one's choosing.

8) The *right to transfer* usage rights of information owned by the legal person to another person for a determinable period or specified purpose.

9) The *duty to prevent harm*: the owner or the user must not use the information to cause harm.

10) *Liability of execution*: to be liable for any harm caused by the usage of information.

In addition, there are some derivative questions that can also be asked:

1) Does this system and data capture value or add value for the business? If not, eliminate it.

2) Is the ownership if this information with another person or persons? If yes, eliminate the information.

3) If it is strictly necessary for the business to store, process and transmit information owned by another person or persons to deliver or capture value, then what are the limits of the business's usage rights?

4) What expressed permission does the business have for the system/data from the owners of the information?

5) How is this information protected by the operational unit?

In fact, the operational manager can refer to the General Data Protection Regulation's (GDPR) implemented by the EU in 2016, and widely considered the benchmark for data privacy at present, to determine the standards of cybersecurity to be applied. Although GDPR is concerned only with information about a natural person, remember that a business is a *legal person* that shares many of the rights and obligations of a natural person. The rules set out in GDPR will set very high standards for any business in its consideration of cybersecurity.

Earlier the problems of social media platforms revealed that the *legal person* that owns these platforms face a dilemma: to facilitate freedom of expression on its platforms but to see it being abused for hate speech, fake news and the likes. The *legal person* rightfully claims that the platform is facilitating freedom of expression: a fundamental human right.

However, the philosophical argument for freedom of expression is much more complex than the three words in popular discourse: *Freedom of expression* is claiming the right to have an opinion, and the right to express that opinion. However, claiming the right to have an opinion provides no guarantee that it is a good opinion and that the opinion has been thoughtfully reasoned and argued for.

Thus, to claim the right to freedom of expression is to also claim the right to be mocked and the right to be ridiculed if it is a poorly reasoned idea. This is a philosophical system designed for exploring ideas, in order to discard those that don't stand up to scrutiny and to acclaim those that do. The expression 'The right to freedom of expression' should always be stated in its complete form: The right to freedom of expression comes with the right to be mocked and ridiculed for poorly reasoned opinions and right to receive acclaim for thoughtful opinions (J.S. Mill[95]).

Just as a natural person can claim the right to freedom of expression and freedom to be mocked and ridiculed, so can the *legal person* and its trustees claim the same right to scrutinise opinions that are expressed on its social media platform, to call out those that are poorly reasoned, falsehood, fake news and hate speech for what they are. In fact, the trustees of the *legal person* can and must claim the right to mock and ridicule poorly reasoned expressions of opinion. The technology for this exists already.

University of Cambridge researchers demonstrated that the problem of hate speech can be contained using artificial intelligence and machine learning, to display a message to the user who is trying to capture an opinion that can be classified as hate speech, and to display a warning to anyone who consumes that message that it might be hate speech[96]. The technology does not interfere with the right to freedom of expression but educate both the author of the opinion and the readers that it might contain hate speech.

It is conceivable that the same technology can be used to identify poorly reasoned ideas, those that come about because of cognitive biases. Biases and prejudices can be easily identified by applying Aristotelian rules on defeating the sophists[97]. In the same way as hate speech is flagged, a popup could be used to warn the poster that he or she is guilty of sophistry and later, to warn the consumer that the post is poorly reasoned.

A New Doctrine of Cybersecurity Risk Management

The proposed organisational model shifts the mindset of the leadership from being agents of shareholders to becoming trustees of the business, a *legal person*. Furthermore, the leadership gives up their monopoly on control by abandoning Taylor's doctrine in favour of a new doctrine of distributed control and mutual accountability. The new doctrine encourages the construction of the organisation - including its cybersecurity practices - around the viable systems model, which releases every employee to seek out advantage for the *legal person* whilst exercising its rights and being responsible for its obligations.

Applying the theories, methodologies and methods of ESG businesses on cybersecurity practices will produce a positive reinforcing feedback loop shown in the dashed line in Figure 18

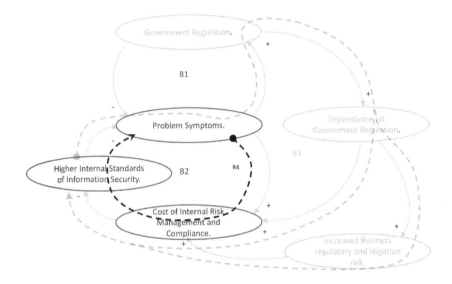

Figure 18   Positive Reinforcing Feedback Loop

Control of and accountability for standards of cybersecurity is set in the operational units, triggering the positive reinforcing feedback loop R4. The shadow of government and regulatory control will continue so the flow direction of the force in reinforcing feedback loop R3 is the same as before, but the strength of that force is reduced over time:

1) Higher standards in cybersecurity will produce fewer symptoms.
2) Fewer symptoms will reduce intervention from the regulator.
3) Less intervention from the regulator will reduce dependence on government intervention.
4) Operating above regulatory standards reduces the risk of litigation and fines to the business.
5) Reducing addiction to regulatory standards reduces the cost of risk management and compliance.

6) Less interference from risk management and compliance increases standards of cybersecurity in the operational units.
7) This triggers the reinforcing loop R4 to produce less symptoms
8) Reducing risk management and compliance costs motivates the operational unit to raise standards.

A curious thing happens to the dilemma the board faced explained on page 143. Boards that subscribe to Friedman's doctrine had to decide between spending on cybersecurity reducing shareholder value or taking a risk on future shareholder value. Making the decision in consideration of the rights and obligations of the *legal person* dissolves the dilemma.

This enquiry has demonstrated here that a cybersecurity management system based on hard systems frameworks and imposed on the business have the tendency to shift the burden of standards of cybersecurity away from the operational units, causes an addiction to regulatory and compliance requirements, and will cost the business more in risk management and compliance.

These costs are likely to grow significantly if the business does not change. Internal friction between operational units, risk management and compliance, and auditing causes inefficiency and is ineffective.

This problem cannot be solved by more technology, larger risk management and compliance teams, or more security controls enforced by internal audit. The answer lies in an ESG approach which understands and confronts the ethical and moral consequences of poor standards in cybersecurity and its potential harm to society.

CHAPTER 18

Comparing ESG and Conventional Businesses

You cannot kindle a fire in any other heart
until it is burning in your own.

Eleanor Doan

So, let's briefly contrast conventional businesses and ESG businesses. Conventional businesses are inclined to regulate the business through codified morals: policies, practices and standards. These codified morals are developed and maintained by:

- Laws codified by governments
- Regulatory requirements
- International standards organisations
- Industry associations that develop standards frameworks and best practices

This has given rise to a whole industry of business consultants that help conventional businesses to navigate the ever increasingly complex regulatory rules, particularly when they operate in multiple countries.

Conventional businesses deploy *first order systems thinking* or *hard systems thinking*, which is the application of Taylor's scientific method to reduce the business to its functions, processes and tasks. It creates a top-down command-and-control system around Responsibility, Accountability, Consulted and Informed (RACI) matrices where management decides what and how something is done, and employees execute within a rigid framework. Employee performance is enumerated and measured through key performance indicators. Employees are extrinsically motivated by the setting of measurable performance targets. Hiring practices focus on hiring for skills, ability and past achievements.

Conventional businesses focus on how an employee will fit into a set process imposing an unrealistic level of specialisation and expertise on candidates. Employees must operate within a narrowly defined role, and worryingly, leave their personal values at the door. In a conventional company, it is the leadership that decides the corporate culture, and from this, defines corporate values and then embarks on a programme of education to transform the business. The hiring process often invokes profiling tests to determine if candidates will fit the culture of the organisation. It seems a lot like an unethical process where the hiring manager claims the moral right to design personalities.

In contrast, ESG businesses are more likely to organise around a soft systems model such as Stafford Beer's, Viable System Model[98]. The Viable Systems Model embraces Ashby's law of requisite variety, that only variety can absorb variety. In the Viable Systems Model, control is distributed applying the Decide, Consult and Informed (DCI) matrix and accountability is mutual: everyone is accountable to everyone else for their performance. The Viable Systems Model embraces the principle that every employee is a trustee for the *legal person* and takes responsibility for its rights and obligations.

The Viable Systems Model is fundamentally humanist in that it encourages individuals to bring their authentic selves to the workplace. Hiring practices are based around values and talent: having ability and a desire to grow. Of course, skills and capabilities are important, but prior achievements are considered less important.

Furthermore, employees are encouraged to grow, intrinsically motivated by their personal values and a shared purpose rather than artificial competition based on enumerated tasks. Hiring is based on enriching teams through diversity and inclusivity. Diversity means differences in gender, age, education, ethnicity, sexuality and familial history amongst others. Combining diverse worldviews to create a team where everyone is valued for their differences fires up innovation and generates collaboration and the pursuit of shared purpose.

Conventional businesses operate with costly internal friction that comes from the separation of responsibility and accountability into different functions. In contrast, ESG companies work in a dynamic frictionless system where control is distributed to where it can be most effective, that responds positively to changes in employees, teams, the business, its markets and society. ESG companies are always ready to take advantage of new opportunities and are more likely to survive long-term in a volatile, uncertain, complex and ambiguous world.

SECTION SEVEN

REWIRING BUSINESS FOR GOOD

Change is inevitable, change is constant.

Benjamin Disraeli

CHAPTER 19

Towards New Doctrines in Business

To challenge the status quo and to go further and move from risks to opportunities, businesses need to look beyond the imperative of short-term profit. For the private sector, everything will start when leaders understand that the purpose of a company is not solely to generate 'fake' short-term profits for shareholders.

Phillip Joubert, Chair of the prince of Wales Corporate Leadership Group

Let's broaden the scope again to a general view of ethics and morals. The analysis and conclusions reached in the enquiry of the implications of the 4th Competitive Force on cybersecurity applies equally to all other dimensions touched by ethics and morals. The discussion of ESG companies came near full circle on page 211, but let's recap some of the conclusions reached.

In many cases businesses are ditching Friedman's doctrine by declaring an approach that will work for the benefit of all stakeholders. This is an important decision, but it floats on nothing and in many cases, it's going to depend on unreliable value judgements. ESG leaders will avoid this by anchoring their decision on an axiom that the business is a *legal person* much like a natural person, and shares many of the rights and obligations of the natural person. Business leaders, managers, shareholders, employees, customers, suppliers and the community will judge the good behaviour of the *legal person*, just like they judge the good behaviour of a natural person. Doing this will make the *legal person* a trusted, reliable and much-admired member of society. Hence business is emphatically an exercise in ethics and morals.

Replacing Friedman's doctrine is not enough. Businesses must also abandon Taylor's doctrine in favour of the viable systems model to unlock the intrinsic motivation of all employees, to give a reasonable amount of autonomy to decide how to exercise the rights and be responsible for the obligation of the *legal person* under any given circumstance. Furthermore, accompanying the autonomy businesses must deploy a system of distributed leadership enabling personal, team and corporate leadership.

It should be acknowledged that changing from hard systems thinking to soft systems thinking will be challenging for most leaders and managers. Hard systems thinking has been around for some 80 years and theories, methodologies and methods have been taught and applied in control frameworks in businesses around the world for decades. Hard systems thinking no longer serves society, the business and everyone touched by it. Businesses that want to remain viable in the long term will have to change, but doing so means going through a process of unlearning as well as a process of learning the new paradigm.

Some might feel that the shareholders have been painted in an unpleasant colour and have been ousted from the new doctrines. This view is wrong. Shareholders are just other natural persons or *legal persons*. Moreover, as natural or *legal persons*, investors carry the same duty of care towards society. Investors play a vital role in the transformation program and their interests are equal to that of supplier, customers, employees and communities.

When looking at ESG companies one sees a holy alliance forming up and down the value chain, with suppliers, with customers, with investors, with communities and with society in general. This presents the biggest threat to businesses that have not yet abandoned Friedman's and Taylor's doctrines. This threat might be behind Phillip Joubert's (Fellow at Cambridge Institute for Sustainable Leadership) claims that if businesses have not already changed, then they are already dead. Mark Carney (Bank of England) with a focus on carbon fuels thinks there is still time[99], but the time to start changing is now. Businesses must abandon Friedman's and Taylor's doctrines now!

The advantages and benefits for ESG businesses are clear, and investors have taken note. The 4th Competitive Force has turned around and businesses are competing for social good: to do good for the environment, for society, for employees, for customers, for suppliers and for investors. The 4th Competitive Force has turned into a force for good.

CHAPTER 20

A Viable Systems Model Strategy for Cybersecurity

At some point we must move from a largely conceptual enquiry to demonstrate a transition to a viable systems model and how it plays out in the transformation of the cybersecurity management system of a business. Let's now consider a fictitious company to see how to build a transformation programme from a hard systems model to a soft systems model using Viable Systems Model.

The purpose of this section is to give a feel of how one might go about constructing a strategy for implementing the Viable Systems Model. Although many of the facts described here relate to real businesses that have gone through this process, these facts have been changed mostly through the aggregation of the case studies to hide the identities of the businesses. As such there may be aspects of cybersecurity that has not been touched.

Case Study Company Context

The bank operates in 20 countries for retail and corporate banking as well as a further 30 countries for private and investment banking. The financial industry is perhaps the most regulated industry in every country. Typically, the standards for cybersecurity is set by the requirement to be compliant with the financial regulators and the laws on data privacy in some 20 countries. In addition to regulatory and legal requirements, the bank has a contractual obligation with Visa and Mastercard to comply with PCI DSS.

This is a considerable undertaking and inevitably, driven by the 4th Competitive Force, the minimum requirements set by the regulators became the maximum the business will do. The bank has followed the conventional approach over the last three decades and have implemented a cybersecurity management system that follows hard systems thinking. Consequently, the bank has an ever-growing cybersecurity risk management team consisting of some one thousand analysts.

There are also several indicators that the bank suffers from the shifting the burden problem and a demonstrable addiction to regulatory standards and risk management frameworks. The cybersecurity team, however, realises that compliance will not protect the business against a cyberattack. This has been confirmed by several simulated target attack exercises against critical banking systems.

Clearly the bank must shift the burden back to the operational managers in each of the business units. Senior management recognizes that there will be some resistance to change and that some operational managers and some members of the risk management team will have to unlearn ways of thinking that have been around for decades.

Financial institutions are perhaps the most targeted by cyber-criminals and nation states because 'that is where the money is'. The bank captures, stores, transmits and processes personal identifiable data (PII) and financial data, bringing into play GDPR which is yet another cybersecurity framework.

Non-compliance will result in regulatory fines and/or restricted access or trading constraints being enforced by the regulators in certain markets. Confirmed breaches will also result in fines and sanctions that will cause serious financial harm to the business, not to speak of reputational, operational and legal risk associated with an actual breach.

Vision and the Goals for Standards in Cybersecurity

The strategy is to transform the business to pursue the highest standards in cybersecurity at every level of operations and management and to secure all business systems, data and networks for each of the operational units. The new control system must be agile in its ability to support the business in its mission to be the leading bank in its chosen markets through product innovation, particularly in market disruption through digitization. The goal for the strategy is to reach a measurable state where the entire organisation is ready and prepared to deal with cybersecurity incidents effectively and efficiently in order to limit harm to the business.

Cybersecurity Governance

The Current State of Cybersecurity Governance and Management

The drive for cybersecurity improvements comes from the CEO and the Group Chief Cybersecurity Officer (CISO). There is a significant budget and commitment at board level for a security transformation programme aimed at updating and securing systems and networks. At this level there is total buy-in. Most of the budget will be spent in the Shared Technology Services Group which provides infrastructure services and security operations for the whole enterprise.

However, the bank is a complex organization operating in some 20 markets with at least 50 operational units. Each of these operational units has its own Business Cybersecurity Officer (BISO) with a reporting line into the Group CISO and into the COO for each business unit.

The individual operational units often have unique regulatory requirements or operate unique systems and networks storing, processing and transmitting financial and personal information. The operational unit BISOs are responsible and accountable for the trust in the confidentiality, availability and integrity of these business-specific systems. Furthermore, the BISO for each operational unit is responsible for making sure the business unit complies with legal and regulatory requirements.

The operational managers for each business unit have control of the budget and tend not to have the same appetite as the group for spending on cybersecurity. The predictable and somewhat reasonable objection is that they have better things to do with the money and that security is a shared services problem.

Operational Managers tend not to demonstrate the same understanding of the importance of cybersecurity risk, or an understanding that regulatory compliance is there to ensure the business applies minimum standards in cybersecurity. Hence, it is sometimes viewed as a tick-box exercise to be completed as cheaply and as quickly as possible. Driven by the 4th Competitive Force they have clearly shifted the burden to Shared Technology Services.

Consequently, the cybersecurity team members are compelled to impose security requirements and remediation projects on the operational units. This will often disrupt the business, drive inefficiency and result in ineffective risk reduction, and hence will create friction within the business.

The Future Operating Model for Cybersecurity

The Enterprise Cybersecurity Policy (ECSP) will develop a cybersecurity operating model that follows the Viable Systems Model by implementing a system of distributed control and mutual accountability. The goal is to encourage the operational units to overcome their resistance to investing in cybersecurity. Cybersecurity management will be fully engaged with and will extend a certain level of autonomy to the operational units. Operational managers can shape the implementation of security controls to align with their own business development strategies, efficiency improvement programmes and its agile response to market changes.

Group Level Governance

Critical to the success of the target operating model are changes to the ECSP that gives control to the operational unit managers and makes them mutually accountable for the security of the systems, data and networks under their control. The operational managers will also be required to report the effectiveness of the cybersecurity standards of the operational unit to the group risk management and compliance committee and to the group CISO. Operational managers will also report to all other operational managers to instil a culture of transparency and honesty. Moreover, operational unit managers will be accountable for the consequences of data breaches within their units.

The ECSP will mandate the establishment of a group level cybersecurity team that will act as advisors to the operational managers of the business units and to regulate their security behaviour to ensure consistency with the business goals for standards of cybersecurity. The group cybersecurity function will act as advisors, consultants and subject matter experts to the operational managers.

Management Processes

Change happens with people first so the group cybersecurity team will put in place a cybersecurity training programme that helps the operational managers of the different business units take fundamental ownership of the security of the systems under their control. Operational managers will each develop a reasonable level of cybersecurity literacy and understanding of the threats to their systems, networks and data.

The culture should be such that the operational managers view the cybersecurity professionals in the business as an internal consulting team to advise on the necessary security controls specific to their systems. As such each operational unit will develop, with advice from the cybersecurity team, a security profile unique to the operational unit but consistent with the goals of the business. Where needed, the cybersecurity team will bring in independent subject matter experts to advise on security controls such as identity and access management, encryption at rest and in transit, and specify the requirements for any technologies that enable this. To facilitate this the cybersecurity team will view cybersecurity management frameworks as valuable catalogues from which they can select controls appropriate for the unique profile for an operational unit.

The operational management training programme will be based on the NIST CSF and will cover the five core functions: identify, protect, detect, respond and recover. The level of training will enable the operational managers to ask important and relevant questions on each of the functions, solicit the right technical expertise from internal and external security consultants, and choose security solutions that are efficient and effective to their specific operational unit.

In doing this, the business will implement an enterprise wide cybersecurity policy that makes it clear that the operational managers have fundamental control and is mutually accountable. The aim is to:

- Align operational unit standards of cybersecurity with the business goals for cybersecurity standards.
- Support risk management by enabling operational management control over the necessary security controls that will mitigate risks for that operational unit.
- Reduce the impact of security breaches on information resources for that operational unit and the potential impact of a cyberattack on the wider enterprise.
- Improve resource management by efficiently managing cybersecurity skills, knowledge and infrastructure and, in particular, view the cybersecurity team as an important resource, and not as a function to which the operational managers can shift the burden of responsibility for cybersecurity.

The ECSP will lay down the policies to develop a cybersecurity culture which builds five values: transparency, mutual accountability, appropriate systems knowledge, compliance with policies and procedures, and formal communications channels. The emphasis for the enterprise is to train the leadership at operational management level in cybersecurity literacy. Furthermore, the training will make the operational managers aware of the impact of a breach not just for their business unit but also for the wider enterprise, and society as a whole. The training will enable the operational managers to be able to brief senior leaders on the standards of cybersecurity in their operational units.

The operational managers can be won over by making them aware of some of the wider benefits of taking responsibility and being mutually accountable for cybersecurity:

- Increased predictability of business operations.

- Greater control over the confidentiality, integrity, and availability of the systems, data and networks under their control.
- Improvements in mitigating risk.
- More cost-effective allocation of security resources.
- Improvements in risk management, business processes, and effective incident response in the case of a breach.
- The ability to make critical decisions based on clear, valid information.
- Greater safeguarding of sensitive information during important business activities.
- Reduced overall costs of risk management and compliance.
- A greater level of autonomy to decide what is best for the operational unit.

CHAPTER 21

Strategic Goals for Cybersecurity

The cybersecurity strategy will:

1) Transform the entire business into a cybersecurity conscious business at every level, from ordinary users through operational management and senior management levels (Role responsibility shown in brackets):

   • Update the cybersecurity user awareness programme to foster full engagement through awareness of the trustee role each employee plays and the responsibility to exercise the rights and be accountable for the liabilities of the business as a *legal person*. (CISO).

   • Develop and run a cybersecurity training course that will build a reasonable level of cybersecurity literacy and to equip operational managers with the knowledge and understanding of their responsibility to secure the systems, data and networks under their control.

   • Implement a reporting system that embeds mutual accountability and that promotes sharing of ideas and standards across operational units, the cybersecurity team and the risk management committee.

(Group Cybersecurity team, reported by the operational manager for each business unit).

2) Establish clear responsibility and mutual accountability for Cybersecurity with operational management.

- Review the Enterprise Cybersecurity Policy (ECSP) to address assignment of Decision, Consulted and Informed matrices for systems, data and networks for each of the operational units and its functions (Group CISO and Board of Directors).
- The ECSP will abandon the RACI matrix and replace it with the DCI matrix and assign accordingly:
- **Decision Maker**: Operational management who makes the decision and is accountable for its impact on the business. Decisions must be made with the principle of being a trustee for the *legal person*, to exercise its rights and be responsible for its obligations. Operational management will be held accountable for liabilities caused by bad decisions.
- **Consulted**: Cybersecurity team accountable for providing guidance based on functional expertise and experience, highlighting issues and raising alternatives to support the Decision Maker.
- **Informed:** Other operational teams, cybersecurity team and risk management committee are notified after the decision has been made and who will need to support the execution of the decision.

The board will agree a CDI matrix to transfer cybersecurity control to the operational units.

3) Establish cybersecurity goals, reporting standards and management reporting structures.

- Agree a standard measure for risk based on the NIST CSF (Identify, Protect, Detect, Response, Recover and reporting frequencies (CISO).
- Agree a reporting line between operational units and to group risk management and cybersecurity management. The Cybersecurity team to produce a consolidated report to the board of directors (CISO and Board).
- Advise operational units on a cybersecurity profile based on NIST CSF unique to each operational unit. (CISO)

4) Establish a best in class cybersecurity expert team that attracts the best cybersecurity analysts and subject matter experts:

- Create an environment that will attract and retain the best in class cybersecurity professionals (CISO).
- Establish a working relationship between the cybersecurity team as consultants (CISO and IS Team) and the operational managers responsible for the security of the systems, data and networks.

5) Identify the best in class information external security consultancies and establish partnerships:

- Review vendor panel and replace under-performing vendors on an annual basis (CISO).
- Implement a system of periodic rotation of vendors.
- Build partnerships that benefit the bank and its chosen vendors (CISO).

6) Collaborate with industry-specific cybersecurity organizations for sharing best practices and information on threats, as well as their tools, techniques and procedures.

- Join organisation like FS-ISAC and participate in conferences and information-sharing platforms (CISO and SOC/CSIRT).
- Enable internal security consultants to participate in cybersecurity events and professional bodies.
- The security team must undertake further industry specific education and be encouraged and supported to engage in continuous professional development (CISO).

7) Build and deploy an alert and focused security operations and CSIRT capability to deal with cyber events effectively and quickly.

- Procure and deploy best in class technology for detecting cybersecurity events (CISO).
- Procure and deploy best in class technology for containing and investigating incidents (SOC/CSIRT).
- Provide access to continuous technical training and skills and capability improvements for the CSIRT teams (CISO and SOC manager).
- Establish an effective threat intelligence function that is fully engaged with operational management.
- Establish a system of mutual accountability with the operational management through incident response playbooks that are developed by them with support from the CSIRT and SOC teams.

Measure Effectiveness and Efficiency

Measuring effectiveness of security controls (its ability to mitigate risk) and confirm efficiency (cost effectiveness) of the standards in cybersecurity.

1) The operational units to measure and report on the efficacy of risk mitigation processes and technologies:

    a. Perform periodic effectiveness assessment using the NIST CSF cybersecurity framework for each of the systems, data and networks of the operational units as agreed in its unique cybersecurity profile. Measure the efficiency of each of the security controls deployed by the operational unit.

    b. The operational unit must perform a gap assessment against each operational unit's legal and compliance requirements.

    c. Engage in persistent trusted third-party security assurance testing (penetration testing) to identify misconfigurations, poor patch management and vulnerabilities in systems, applications and networks including the technology deployed to protect these.

    d. Engage in full end-to-end threat-intelligence-lead simulated targeted attack and response technical assessment performed on a persistent basis to assess the identify, protect, detect, response and recover functions of each operational unit. Specific measurements will include time-to-detect and time-to-remediate.

    e. Perform tabletop CSIRT exercises led by the operational unit managers on a quarterly basis to assess the response, recovery and reporting processes in the organization.

2) Measure the efficiency of risk mitigation and present in financial terms.

    a. Measure the efficiency of the security controls and its ability to be agile and supportive of business functions and new business development initiatives.

b. Measure and review the efficiency of the security technologies, along with determining planned obsolescence and the renewal plan.

c. Measure the efficiency of the cybersecurity team compared to their contribution to the standards of cybersecurity. Identify and eliminate friction that might arise between operational managers and the cybersecurity team members.

Implement a reporting system that supports mutual accountability so operational report on effectiveness and efficiency to other operational managers, the group risk committee and the group CISO on an agreed periodic basis.

User Awareness of Cybersecurity

In the *current operating model*, the bank employs comprehensive user level cybersecurity training during the on-boarding process for new employees. Users must complete this training (including a comprehensive background check) before they receive privileges including access to sensitive data. Training including phishing awareness, data privacy policies, data handling policies, and computer and mobile phone fair use policies.

The training is delivered through online portals and assessed and tracked to ensure employees engage with the material. Simulated phishing campaigns are periodically launched to measure employee awareness of social engineering attacks via emails, followed up with compulsory/mandatory further training for those who click on links. All employees must repeat the online training programmes every two years. However, the training is often bullet list based with multi choice questions to test understanding.

In the *future operating model*, a new training programme will be developed using storytelling to make it more effective, and to develop a fundamental understanding that users are trustees for the business as a *legal person* and as trustees must exercise its rights and be responsible for its obligations.

Transferring Level of Control

Identify: Critical Systems, Data and Networks

In the *current operating model,* the process of identifying the critical business systems is managed by the cybersecurity team. As such it is likely to be incomplete and the operational managers may not have a complete understanding of their systems, data and networks, and the security controls around these. The following provides a summary overview of the systems, data and networks in the business.

The Critical Systems of this organization are its 20 core banking systems servicing 20 different markets. The core banking systems stores personal identifiable information (PII) and financial data. This is a prime target for cyber criminals targeting financial institutions with the purpose of defrauding the bank and its customers. These systems represent a reputational and litigation risk in this intensely regulated industry.

A second set of critical systems are the payment card management (PCM) systems of which there are more than 30. Regulators are increasingly demanding that these systems must be managed in accordance with PCI DSS.

The inter-bank settlement systems including SWIFT are also considered to be critical to the bank's operations and are vulnerable to attack specifically because they support very large payments and therefore will give access to significant funds to a cybercriminal.

Finally, the transaction banking systems such as the online banking, corporate banking and open banking systems (Open Application Programming Interfaces API) provided to corporate customers provide access to the PII and Financial data from outside the bank's internal networks, and so is critical to the bank's mission.

The Critical Network of the organization is the internal network supporting 50,000 workstations and thousands of shared servers and core banking platforms. Until recently this was a flat network meaning that if a cyber attacker gained access to one workstation, (s)he would have full visibility of the entire network.

The flat network is a critical vulnerability that is being urgently addressed through a programme of network segregation / segmentation. This is a work-in-progress managed by the cybersecurity team.

In the target operating environment, the operational managers will take ownership, be responsible and mutually accountable for the segregation and protection of the networks under their control. This is a challenging task if you consider the many systems, workstations and markets. It is made more complex by imposing PCI DSS standards on the network.

Another network is the one that connects the web services (for online banking) to the core banking systems. The technology is old and therefore difficult to secure so mitigating controls will be required to protect this network.

The Critical Data the organization stores and transmits includes personal identifiable information, online banking credentials, financial data and payment card data. Loss of this information could give rise to identity theft and the theft of financial assets.

Banks are already rich targets and the introduction of online banking and mobile banking has given access to these systems and networks to devices outside of the banks' control. The last five years have seen significant developments in access and authentication processes in online and mobile banking to ensure that transactions are properly validated through a multi-factor authentication process.

A challenge for the security team is 'toxic data'. Toxic data is where individual users or small teams copy personal identifiable information and payment card data onto their works stations for legitimate processing, but leave it unencrypted and with no identity and access controls in place besides their own user credentials for accessing workstations. This is a critical vulnerability, but imposing security controls in many cases prevents users from performing their legitimate jobs. Striking a balance between security and access in these cases will be challenging.

In the *future operating model,* the operational units will identify the systems, data and networks under its control. It is also not clear that any form of technology governance has been applied. The operational units will follow the advice of the cybersecurity team to assess the data and technology under their control following the governance guidelines laid out in the ECSP.

Protective Measures

Physical Access Control

The bank will lay down a policy in the ECSP that sets the goals for physical access control that ensures the deployment of the following access control technology:

1) Every office must be equipped with badge access control gates that prevent tailgating. Entry and exit must be logged and correlated with workstation sign-in logs by the security

operations centre who must follow up with appropriate and agreed response processes.

2) Designated sensitive areas such as data centres must have additional biometric authentication access gates allowing entry only to designated personnel.

3) All entry and exit points must have security cameras that record access on a continuous 24-hour basis stored for 6 months.

4) Data networks cannot be extended into the public areas beyond the physical access control barriers.

5) Physical access control must be assessed periodically, as defined in the ECSP and standards reported to risk management and the CISO.

6) The physical access control system must be on separate protected network from the corporate network to prevent it from being compromised via the corporate network.

Network Protection

The ECSP will define the policies with goals for standards for network protection for each operational unit. The following will be considered:

1) The operational unit must protect every internet access point with a suitable firewall configured to allow access to necessary connections only. The operational managers must periodically verify that it is configured correctly. The firewall must be effective in protecting access to the network from the internet.

2) The operational unit must apply effective network segregation of the networks use by different business functions.

3) Effective segregation can be achieved by deploying the enterprise standard for software defined networks with support and advise from the shared technology services function.

4) Every network must deploy network access control systems that will prevent alien devices from being plugged into the network.

5) Every network device must have logging capability and the logs must be collected by the Security Operations Centre.

6) Every network must deploy intrusion detection systems and the logs must be collected and transmitted to the SIEM.

7) The operational unit will deploy DDoS protection on all its web applications and web services.

User Identity and Access management

The ECSP will lay down goals for identity and access management (IAM) and the shared technology services function will select and provide suitable technology. The operational unit will:

1) Enable two-factor authentication and must be deployed group-wide.

2) Deploy IAM as a single sign-on for all systems used by the operational units.

3) Deploy IAM to enable granular access defined by user roles (Role Based Access Control). This must be fully integrated in all systems and applications used by the operational units in line with group policies.

Client Identity and Access Management

The ECSP will lay down the cybersecurity goals for online and mobile applications which may include the following.

1) The online banking applications must use two-factor authentication for both retail and corporate clients. A second level of authentication must be implemented to authorize setting up new beneficiaries and transactions.

2) Mobile applications must have a security certificate deployed on the device to allow for certain transaction types. The application must deploy root or jailbreak detections on devices as well as attached debugger detection. Furthermore, the mobile applications must be bound to a specific device during installation.

Data Protection

The ECSP will lay down the goals for data encryption in transit and at rest as follows:

1) All data in transit must be encrypted with HTTPS for online banking applications.
2) All systems that store and process PII must transmit and store data encrypted.
3) Data at rest must be hardware encrypted.
4) Apply effective access management technology to protect data from unauthorized access that might impact availability, integrity or confidentiality.
5) Apply tools that detect the presence of 'toxic' data: sensitive data that is located on unprotected file servers, user workstation or laptops.

Legal and Compliance Matters

The operational unit manager will employ a suitably qualified person to identify the legal requirements imposed by the respective governments under local data protection acts, data privacy acts, regulatory requirements, etc. The operational manager will develop management processes to deal with these requirements which may include the following:

1) The relevant contact details and requirements for reporting a breach of sensitive data as defined under the relevant local laws: Data Protection Commissioner, the Police cybercrimes unit, etc.
2) The definition of sensitive data that falls under the reporting regime.
3) The trigger points for notifying the authorities of a security breach.
4) The job role within the operational unit responsible for reporting breaches.
5) The action dictated by law following a breach, such as informing the affected customers in case of PII breach; the actions required to protect the privacy of the affected people; the compensation policy required under law.
6) The steps the operational unit must take to prevent a security breach.
7) The steps the operational unit must take to process certain requests from the customer, whose information is stored transmitted and processed, such as giving full access to the information held on the person, delete or transfer data to another party and the accuracy of data.
8) The financial penalties that can be imposed on the business for non-compliance or failure to secure the sensitive data.
9) The permissible geolocations of the sensitive data for each of the operational units, for instance, the banking regulator in some countries do not permit any data to be stored outside of their jurisdiction. Also called data sovereignty.
10) Develop the reporting processes to notify senior management of a breach.
11) Ensure that these requirements are incorporated in the CSIRT playbooks and decision trees and are rehearsed on a periodic basis.

The operational manager must report these measures in the standard, formal reporting system.

CHAPTER 22

Detect, Respond and Recover in Ten Steps

The operational units must develop a complete understanding of, and be able to report on, its incident response and readiness.

Step 1: Prevention

In the current operating model, the business has centralised control and shared services has responsibility for all prevention controls. It has a comprehensive firewall protecting the internal network, deployed end-point protection tools, anti-virus tools, build standards and hardening of devices, build standards and hardening of application and files servers, two-factor authentication and access control, network access control, and patch management.

The bank performs regular (at least annual) security assessments to verify configuration standards and hardening of systems. All web and mobile applications are penetration tested by an external trusted vendor and all identified vulnerabilities must be fixed and verified fixed before applications go live. The bank performs user awareness training and quarterly phishing training for all employees.

The bank's internal network is flat so that any one of the 50,000 workstations and laptops has access to the entire corporate network. This is a recognized vulnerability which is currently undergoing a transformation project through the implementation of software definable network technology that will segregate countries, business units and business functions.

The future operating model will distribute control to the operational units and implement mutual accountability.

Step 2: Planning

The bank operates in around 20 countries with each country having 1 to 4 business units (investment and private banking, retail banking, corporate banking, and mortgages).

Central CSIRT

The Central CSIRT is within the shared technology services (STS) function and reports to the STS CISO who in turn reports into the Group CISO. The following central roles form part of the CSIRT.

- STS CISO
- CSIRT Team of CSIRT and SOC
- Network Control Engineer
- Head of network administration for the corporate network
- Heads of systems administrators for shared systems
- Operational Managers for shared services
- CIO for shared IT services.
- A permanent team of some 30 security experts including digital forensics and incident response certified analysts and consultants
- In-house legal counsel
- In-house public relations

- Contracted incident response teams from several trusted vendors with specialist knowledge

In the target operating model CSIRT will follow the distributed control and mutual accountability principles of the viable systems model.

Distributed CSIRT

The operational management teams for each of the business units will build an internal CSIRT with the following roles:

- Business unit (BU) CISO
- Network administration for business unit networks
- Systems administrator for each of the systems unique to the business unit
- Head of the business unit
- Functional operations managers
- IT manager

The SOC is part of the STS and therefore normally the first point where a cyberattack is detected (unless it comes from an external source such as discovering sensitive data from the bank is available on the dark web). In the early processes of the response the central CSIRT will pull in the relevant distributed team to participate in the response process.

Step 3: Preparation

Following the SWIFT payment gateway attacks on the Bangladesh Central bank, the SWIFT organization published the SWIFT Security Framework with which all subscribers must comply. Relevant to this scenario are requirements six and seven which states that a subscriber must be able to detect anomalous activity on systems and transactions, and plan for incident response and information sharing. Once the bank remediated security around the SWIFT payments systems (some 20 across the world) the bank commissioned a Threat Intelligence Led Simulated Targeted Attack from a third-party cybersecurity specialist to test the effectiveness of the detect, respond and recovery processes. The red team planned the attacks in line with the tools, tactics and procedures (TTP) of the attackers and executed the attack without the knowledge of the SOC or SWIFT administrators. The red team was successful in executing payment transfers which were detected by the SOC which, in turn, exercised the CSIRT and showed that it was effective.

In the target operating model, the CSIRT of each operational unit will be the responsibility of the operational unit managers and must demonstrate the capability compatible with the central CSIRT.

Step 4: Detection

In the current operating model, the bank has deployed a plethora of technologies to detect an attack. Central to this is a SPLUNK (other products are available) powered SIEM that collect systems logs from all endpoints, servers and network protection devices such as firewalls and routers. Furthermore, the bank uses network intrusion detection technology for detecting anomalous network traffic, and data leakage detection to scan network traffic for sensitive data, such as credit card data being transferred in large volumes. The bank also uses end-point detection technology that looks for changes in the behaviour that could indicate a compromised endpoint.

The bank has recently built a threat-hunting team with specialist knowledge on how the attacker mindset works. The bank now recognizes that technology is not enough and that it is essentially a human problem. The threat-hunting team is focused on finding the unauthorized humans on the network. The SOC is centrally controlled as part of the shared services team. This will continue in the future operating model, but operational management will report on the use case analysis and correlation rules of the systems, data and networks under its control.

Step 5: Analysis.

In the current operating model, the bank has an experienced CSIRT team. On analysing an incident there is comprehensive situational awareness and detailed procedures and playbooks developed with the assistance of experts to, in the first instance determine if this is a technology outage of some kind or that the incident needs to be escalated to the cybersecurity CSIRT team for processing.

The banks have some 300 systems so identifying the systems/data/ networks affected by the incident requires careful analysis and situational awareness. To facilitate this, there is a comprehensive systems directory complete with upstream and downstream interdependences and cross referencing to business units. The Central CSIRT can very quickly determine the systems and the business units so that the relevant Distributed CSIRT are pulled in to deal with the incident.

The systems directory also contains impact analysis so that incidents can be quickly prioritized (functional, informational and recovery), and the most urgent ones dealt with first. The size of the CSIRT and forensics teams means that several incidents can be dealt with simultaneously. Identifying the relevant impact is supported by a threat intelligence team with detailed knowledge of a variety of threats and their tactics, techniques and procedures as well as indicators of compromise (the digital signals that might be on the network or in endpoints when an attacker is active). This is used to determine the type of attack, the potential systems and data being targeted, and pre-planned procedures to contain the attack and to minimize the impact on the business unit.

In the future operating model operational management will be responsible for reporting procedures and playbooks and for periodic rehearsals.

Step 6: Containment

In the current operating model, containment is a significant challenge for the CSIRT team. The bank has a flat network with little control over specific network segments. Thus, being able to isolate a network segment under attack is challenging and in some network attacks almost impossible.

When an attack is suspected on an individual workstation, it is possible for the CSIRT team to disconnect the workstation from the network, and in each office location there is a response team that will track down the location of the device and the person working on it. The person (contractor or employee) is escorted off premises for the duration of the investigation and the workstation is removed and shipped to the forensics laboratory for further enquiry. The forensics laboratory is an isolated network so there is little risk of the infected workstation contaminating anything else in the operational network.

The bank operates 24/7 so in some cases it will be difficult to simply disable online banking services. However, the bank has failover functionality and can bring secondary or backup systems online very quickly, but the decision must be based on where the attack is focused and whether failover will circumvent the attack. For these decisions, there are expert-developed procedures and playbooks with decision trees to facilitate the decision. The central CSIRT has the necessary authority to make these decisions.

In the future operating model network isolation will be resolved once the network segmentation using software definable network technology is completed. Additionally, operational units will report on its networks and how they are protected and how intrusion detection is planned. It will be possible to isolate a network once an intrusion is detected. Authority over decision to isolate networks or system will be redistributed to the operational units with oversight from the central CSIRT.

Step 7: Communication

In the current operating model, the central CSIRT has comprehensive communication and escalation protocols with prepared content on what to communicate to external stakeholders. The communication plan takes into account that the bank operates in 20 markets. Thus, it has complex and interdependent regulatory requirements to report incidents within varying timeframes, triggered by different conditions. The content of each communication has been prepared in advance and requires little editing to incorporate the specifics of the attack.

The Bank incident response and crisis management playbooks assign responsibility to members of the Central CSIRT and where relevant the Distributed CSIRT for communications to relevant regulators, law enforcement and other external stakeholders and affected partners and clients. This includes specific guidance and assigned responsibility for senior management for downwards communications, and for public communications. The content of these communications is largely prepared and requires editing to incorporate specifics where required. The decisions and trigger points for communications are clearly defined.

The CSIRT teams have an established, out-of-bounds communications channel provided by an external incident response contractor. The CSIRT communication system is external to the corporate network and corporate communications systems. The contractor provides the technology and technical support to facilitate horizontal communications between teams.

This will not change in the target operating model, but operational units will report on the quality and completeness of their communication plans.

Step 8: Eradication

Following on from containment and communication, the central cyber defence team has a well-documented and practiced process for dealing with an attack. Containment often means that critical systems must be disabled, or access to critical systems must be disabled to mitigate the impact of an attack. In these cases, the operational managers are an important part of the decision-making process. It is often a difficult decision because disabling a system has an operational impact and therefore impacts on revenue. In some cases, allowing the attack to continue is less expensive than disabling the system.

The tools available to the SOC and CSIRT enables the team to remove access rights for individual employees whose credentials have been hijacked, disable network access for their laptops and workstations. Intrusion Detection Systems are updated with the network indicators of compromise to detect other instances used by the attackers. Firewalls are updated to prevent connections to command-and-control servers outside of the company.

Step 9: Recovery

All critical systems have automatic failover capability so that guarantees continuous processing. However, in banks the attacks are more often than not on the integrity of data. Hackers execute funds transfer transactions and inevitably leave a trail as to where the money went. The banking industry has protocols in place to trace the money and to recover funds with some success, but not all illegitimate funds transfers are recoverable so there are inevitable losses. Fraud is closely related to cybersecurity and the bank has extensive fraud detection and prevention measures which support the cybersecurity objectives.

Banks have a tradition of 24/7 operations with failover and recovery processes that has been expertly developed over decades so cases of most DDoS style attacks normal operations can be restored quickly. Failover tests are run on a monthly basis to ensure they work effectively.

Step 10: Post-event analysis

In the current operating model, the incident response team investigates and reports to management on all cyber and operational incidents with a full enquiry of how the cyberattack occurred including the patient-zero workstation or laptop. The enquiry is performed by the in-house digital forensics and fraud teams and will include a reconstructed timeline, technical details on the vulnerabilities exploited, a review of the security controls that could have prevented the attack, and the detection controls (SOC correlation rules and use cases) that could have alerted the security operations team earlier if that was at all possible. A full remediation program is developed and rolled into the banks ongoing cybersecurity programme to close the vulnerabilities in systems and networks that allowed the attacker through.

The bank will engage with FS-ISAC and shares details of the attack with other members as well as with its threat intelligence providers.

CHAPTER 23

Threat Intelligence

The financial industry is particularly targeted by cyber criminals and some rogue governments. In the first instance, banks perform large volumes and large transfers of money, so organized cybercriminals attack it on a wide front. Firstly, banking Trojan style attacks that target individual client computers to obtain online banking credentials with the view to exfiltrate money from individual accounts. Secondly, ATM Jackpotting attacks are on the rise where attackers target the ATM infrastructure to enable money mules to collect cash from ATM machines on a large scale. In both online banking attacks and ATM attacks, the equipment is in the public domain and largely outside of the physical security controls a bank might normally deploy to protect its assets. Banking Trojans have grown in sophistication to the extent that the banking trojan adapts itself to the specific bank's online banking application on the client computer or smart phone, and a single Trojan can be ready and programmed to attack a multitude of banking applications without requiring manual intervention.

Banks are also susceptible to more sophisticated attacks on payment gateways. Examples include the attack on the Bangladeshi Central Bank in 2016, which targeted the SWIFT payment system, and the attack on Standard Bank also in 2016, which targeted the generic card

The 4th Competitive Force For Good | 179

payment router. In both cases, millions of dollars were stolen before the institutions could take containment action. Whereas online and ATM attacks tend to be attributed to criminal organizations, these payment gateway attacks are believed to have been perpetrated by the Lazarus group which is closely associated with North Korea. Payment gateway attacks demonstrate a level of sophistication and planning that can only be achieved by a well-funded and well-organized group. A payment gateway attack usually starts with the attacker gaining access to a single workstation through phishing or spear-phishing. From there the attacker will escalate privileges and establish persistence on the network. Once persistence is established, the attacker will move laterally and perform reconnaissance to identify the target system. Most payment gateways have extensive anti-fraud detection functionality which the attackers will disable through a modification of the transaction flow before the final attack is executed.

Financial institutions also face significant cyberattacks from nation state threats or nation state sponsored threats. Here, the aim is to cause social disruption and economic harm to the targeted nation, motivated by political or geopolitical differences. Russia or Russian-based threat actors are particularly active in this space, but North Korea is known to have performed a very destructive attack on South Korean banks and TV networks which disabled large numbers of computers in target networks in a sophisticated Distributed Denial of Service (DDoS) attack.

The tactics, techniques and procedures employed by cyber criminals vary a great deal: from emailing Trojans to individual clients to compromise their personal computers or smart phones in order to inject banking Trojans, to stealthy attacks on the internal infrastructure of banks to compromise payment gateways. Operational leaders must take actionable threat intelligence into consideration and must report as part of the reporting structure agreed for and stated in the enterprise cybersecurity policy. The cybersecurity team will establish a threat intelligence team to:

1) Seek out, collate and make actionable the latest threat intelligence.
2) Produce a system that distributes relevant threat intelligence to operational managers.
3) Operational managers to consult with the threat intelligence team on a regular basis and also at any time that a new system, data and network is considered to support business development and/or change.

Concluding the VSM Strategy

The strategy explained for the fictional bank may be developed further, but hopefully it illustrates how a business might go about to distribute control and to create mutual accountability. The strategy reveals how the bank will move from its current governance and operating model to a dynamic viable systems model that does not hamper the operational units' ability to respond to market forces, embeds cybersecurity literacy across the business and makes most of the scarce resource.

CONCLUSION

The impact of Covid-19 on the global economy, societies, communities, and business are already devastating, and at the time of releasing this book the world is not yet in control of the spread and treatment and vaccines were years away. Governments are scrambling to put together plans to resuscitate their economies, but increasingly support for business is coming with conditions attached.

Prior to Covid-19 businesses that wanted to embrace ESG principles were encouraged to try and answer the question 'Why are we here?' The time for businesses to contemplate this question has run out. Covid-19 changed all that. Business behaviour under lockdown is being scrutinised by governments, but most importantly by society at large, by customers, suppliers, employees, and taxpayers.

For too long have businesses succumbed to the 4th Competitive Force and have run within the margins of risk, prioritising efficiency over effectiveness. When Covid-19 spread around the world and the sheer scale of the tragedy it caused became apparent, these businesses could not deal with the economic impact of lockdowns and other measures imposed by governments to save lives. Neither could the people they employed who was forced to live from pay cheque to pay cheque. Neither business nor their employees had any financial resilience. These businesses have run cap in hand to governments for a bailout, but that money must come from somewhere and that somewhere is future generations of taxpayers. Whereas millennials and generation-Z already refuses to work with companies with a single-minded focus on making a profit, future generations are going to ask the hard question of business leaders, employers and producers. That hard question is 'Why are YOU here? Businesses no longer have the time to contemplate the value of becoming ESG companies and to ask the question for themselves. Now is the time for business leaders to think about how they are going to *answer* this question, and it comes at three levels:

The personal Question: Why are you here? As an individual business leader how will you answer this question?

The team question: Why is this team here? Why should society allow this team to run this business? As a leadership team in a business how will you answer this question?

The corporate question? Why is this corporation here? What is it going to do for society, the environment, employees, customers, suppliers, and investors?

What answer can you give that will satisfy a society that had to rescue your business. Why are you here and why should society offer you the privilege of running a business? Your answer must demonstrate an emphatic commitment to a better, more resilient society.

This book has shown how the 4th Competitive Force drives businesses to spend more money on ineffective cybersecurity by prioritising efficiency over efficacy. Business leaders and cybersecurity leaders alike focused on understanding the value of cybersecurity to the shareholders. But cybersecurity is not just a business issue. It is emphatically an issue for society. In the context where cyber means to govern through information cyberattacks puts society at risk when business fail to take the necessary steps to secure the information infrastructure that society has become dependent on. Lockdown has forced many organisations to switch to a telecommuting model putting immense pressure on the information infrastructure that exposes society and the global economy to massive cyberattacks.

The Covid-19 epidemic has created an unprecedented economic crisis that exposed the vulnerability of the capitalist system that embraces Friedman and Taylor's doctrines, but it also offers society a unique opportunity to create a new economic model where businesses and markets are a force for good for society and the environment.

Information is the way in which society is governed. Humans have lived in an information age for as long as humans have been able to communicate. That has always been the case. The information age is not new. Technology has made the system of governance through information more efficient and effective but has also exposed it to attacks from miscreants. This vulnerability is not a problem that is naturally there. It is a vulnerability that was created by the 4th Competitive Force. It can and must be solved.

So, the *why are you here question* must also answer what you are going to do to secure the information infrastructure. How are you going to run your business to protect and secure the information it generates, processes, and stores, to govern the business and its relationship with society, employees, customers, suppliers and investors. To do this the business must move to a viable systems model where control is distributed, and accountability is mutual. The focus of the book was on cybersecurity, but every aspect of the business is subject to the same weaknesses, the shifting the burden problem. As such the viable systems model can be applied broadly throughout the business, resting on an axiom that every employee is a trustee of the legal person, makes judgements on its behalf and is responsible for its obligations to society. This is the new DNA for the business and now is the time to replace Friedman and Taylor's doctrines.

Change starts at the top and will require a relearning and a new theory of business, the trustee theory.

APPENDIX A

ISACA's COBIT 2019 and the Viable Systems Model

It is greatly encouraging that ISACA and the authors of COBIT 2019 (ISACA COBIT 2019 and The NIST CSF Implementation Guide for COBIT 2019[100, 101]) have built the framework around the Viable Systems model. There is some concern that the framework still invokes the RACI matrix so care must be taken to not distribute accountability in such a way as to invoke centralised command and control.

This benchmark document drives a distinction between information and technology as two separate domains that are managed and controlled as equal partners in information technology. Furthermore, it recognizes two important duties of information and technology: Technology captures value in information for the business, and security preserves that value.

The follow-up document also produced by ISACA The NIST CSF implementation guide for COBIT 2019 puts a lot more emphasis on factors that implement the Viable Systems Model. It is worth repeating some here:

- […] determines the scope of systems and assets that support the selected business line or process. The author takes selected business line to mean operational unit.
- […] for the business line (operational unit) or process, the organization identifies related systems and assets, regulatory requirements, and overall risk approach.
- The business/process level, in turn, uses the information as inputs into the risk management process, and collaborates with IT management and IT process owners to communicate business needs.
- the information flow is cyclical, with ongoing monitoring as a critical step.

More significant statements can be found elsewhere in the implementation guide:

- Designing for the end-to-end governance system
- Nearly all enterprises, in some way, are part of critical infrastructure. Each enterprise is connected to critical functions as a consumer through the global economy, telecommunication services and many other ways. Improvements in risk management by each member of this ecosystem cumulatively reinforces the efforts of others, thereby reducing cybersecurity risk globally.
- For some enterprises, a separate risk assessment may be conducted for each business area (e.g., human resources, accounting and customer support) as defined by CSF Step 1: Prioritize and Scope. Separate risk assessments can support separate Target Profiles and ensure that risk specific to each business area is addressed appropriately, without overcompensating. The enterprise wide risk assessment defines a minimum threshold and ensures that less-sensitive business areas are not neglected and not providing avenues of attack for malicious users.

- The Framework can be adapted to support the different business lines or processes within an organization, which may have different business needs and associated risk tolerance.
- The CSF stresses a common language that can be used to communicate requirements among interdependent stakeholders responsible for critical infrastructure products and services. Communication is especially important among stakeholders within the enterprise supply chain.

Thus, COBIT 2019 and the accompanying NIST CSF implementation guide are very valuable resources for businesses that wants to transform to higher standards of cybersecurity built around the viable systems model. Additionally, the implementation guide provides detailed advice on the reporting system around identify, protect, detect, response and recover. The importance of the NIST CSF reporting framework is that it condenses the individual profiles into five measures that can be easily compared, and that will give senior management a simple view of the standards of cybersecurity for the business and for each of the operational units. So, kudos to ISACA, and the authors of the two papers.

ACKNOWLEDGEMENTS

One cannot work in the exciting and brilliant industry that is cybersecurity without engaging with many brilliant consultants that are working hard to make the information world a safer place. I cannot list all the great minds here, but you know who you are.

I must thank Louise Crowe who brilliantly edited the many original drafts, who pointed out the many places where I could provide more robust arguments, and who encouraged me without fail over the last six months.

I also have to thank Harvard University for their brilliant course *Managing Risk in the Information Age* where for the first time I saw a strategy for cybersecurity that fitted with what was still a vague idea I had developed, and Cambridge University for the *High Impact Leadership* course which paved the way for me to explore many of the theories, methodologies and methods I have applied here.

Finally, I owe a gratitude of debt to Ken Hickson from the Hickson Team who copy edited the manuscript and who gave invaluable advice on the structure and flow of the book, as well as direction on how to reflect on the Covid 19 pandemic and its impact and relevance to the enquiry presented here.

NOTES

1. Morgan, S., Cybercrime Damages US$ 6trillion by 2021 https://cybersecurityv___entures.com/hackerpocalypse-cybercrime-report-2016/ (Accesses 11 May 20202)

2. Polgreen L., The Collapse of the Information Ecosystem Poses Profound Risk for Humanity. https://www.theguardian.com/commentisfree/2019/nov/19/the-collapse-of-the-information-ecosystem-poses-profound-risks-for-humanity?CMP=share_btn_wa (Accessed 3 January 2020)

3. Interpol https://www.interpol.int/en/News-and-Events/News/2020/INTERPOL-launches-awareness-campaign-on-COVID-19-cyberthreats

4. Caramela S. Management Theory of Frederic Taylor https://www.business.com/articles/management-theory-of-frederick-taylor/ (Accessed 27 February 2020)

5. Friedman's Doctrine https://en.wikipedia.org/wiki/Friedman_doctrine (Accessed 27 February 2020)

6. Kim D., (1992), Systems Archetypes https://thesystemsthinker.com/wp-content/uploads/2016/03/Systems-Archetypes-I-TRSA01_pk.pdf (Accessed 9 February 2020)

7. Wiener N., Cybernetics: Control and Communications in Animals and Machines, The MIT Press

8. Palmeter 1999. The Ford Pinto Case https://users.wfu.edu/palmitar/Law&Valuation/Papers/1999/Leggett-pinto.html (accessed 15 December 2019)

9. Tracing the Opioid Crisit in the United States https://www.nature.com/articles/d41586-019-02686-2 (accessed 23 January 2020)

10. Elliot L., Zero hours Contract is not Flexibility but exploitation https://www.theguardian.com/business/2016/mar/09/zero-hour-contract-is-not-flexiblity-but-exploitation-and-its-rising (Accessed 8 March 2020)

11. Taleb N., 2008, The Black Swan: The Impact of the Highly Improbable, Penguin.

12. Friedman M., Shareholder Theory https://en.wikipedia.org/wiki/Friedman_doctrine (Accessed 15 December 2019)

13. Friedman M. Shareholder Theory https://en.wikipedia.org/wiki/Friedman_doctrine (Accessed 15 December 2019)

14. Jensen M. Meckling W., Theory of the Firm https://www.sciencedirect.com/science/article/pii/0304405X7690026X (Accessed 1 February 2020)

15. Roach F. Compliance and Risk Management https://assets.corporatecompliance.org/Portals/1/PDF/Resources/past_handouts/Higher_Ed/2009/Sun/P4Roach.pdf

16. Zeballos-Roig, J., Market Insider, Trump Defends Huge Cuts to the CDC... https://markets.businessinsider.com/news/stocks/trump-defends-cuts-cdc-budget-federal-government-hire-doctors-coronavirus-2020-2-1028946602 (Accessed 27 April 2020)

17. George Manbiot, Boris Johnson's US trade deal will make Britain a paradise for disaster capitalists https://www.theguardian.com/commentisfree/2020/jun/09/boris-johnson-trade-deal-us-chlorinated-chicken (Accessed 14 June 2020)

18. Härle P. Havas A. Samandari H. The Future of Bank Risk Management. https://www.mckinsey.com/business-functions/risk/our-insights/the-future-of-bank-risk-management (Accessed 3 January 2020)

19. English S., Hammond S., Cost of Compliance. https://legal.thomsonreuters.com/en/insights/reports/cost-compliance-2017 (Accessed 3 January 2020)

20. Smith A. Great Books of the Western World (ed. Maynard R.) Encyclopaedia Britannica Inc, Chicago. Volume 39

21. Robson, D., How east and west think in profoundly different ways, https://www.bbc.com/future/article/20170118-how-east-and-west-think-in-profoundly-different-ways (Accessed 21 March 2020)

22. Taylor F., Frederick Taylor's Scientific Method https://oer.missouriwestern.edu/rsm424/chapter/frederick-taylors-scientific-management/ (Accessed 3 January 2020)

23. Goldsmith M. What is Science http://www.uefap.com/reading/exercise/tewufs/tewufs1.htm (accessed 23 February 2020)

24. Stewart M., 2009, The Management Myth, WW Norton and Co, New York.

25. Jensen M. Meckling W., Theory of the Firm https://www.sciencedirect.com/science/article/pii/0304405X7690026X (Accessed 1 February 2020)

26. Bower J. Paine S. Managing for the long term. https://hbr.org/2017/05/

managing-for-the-long-term?utm_medium=social&utm_source=linkedin&utm_campaign=hbr (Accessed 3 January 2020.)

27. Hay J. Shareholders Think They Own the Company, They Are Wrong. https://www.ft.com/content/7bd1b20a-879b-11e5-90de-f44762bf9896 (Accessed 3 January 2020)

28. Business Roundtable Redefines the Purpose of a Corporation to Promote 'An Economy That Serves All Americans' https://www.businessroundtable.org/business-roundtable-redefines-the-purpose-of-a-corporation-to-promote-an-economy-that-serves-all-americans (Accessed 23 February 2020)

29. Brenkert G., Beauchamp T. Ed., 2010 The Oxford Handbook to Business Ethics. Oxford University Press, New York (page 702)

30. Burke E., Speech in Bristol http://press-pubs.uchicago.edu/founders/documents/v1ch13s7.html (Accessed 11 March 2020)

31. Brenkert G., Beauchamp T. Ed., 2010 The Oxford Handbook to Business Ethics. Oxford University Press, New York (page 3 and 4)

32. Aristotle. 282-324 BCE, Various readings incl. on logic, physics, metaphysics, defeating the sophist and ethics. Great Books of the Western World (ed. Maynard R.) Encyclopaedia Britannica Inc, Chicago. Volume 8 and 9

33. Bentham J. 1748-1832, An Introduction to the Principles of Morals and Legislation

34. Morgan J., How this CEO is transforming his 22,000person company to focus on social purpose https://thefutureorganization.com/how-this-ceo-is-transforming-his-22000-person-company-to-focus-on-purpose/ (Accessed 7 March 2020)

35. Kant E. 1724-1768, Groundwork of the Metaphysics of Morals, Critique of Practical Reason and Metaphysics of Morals. Great Books of the Western World (ed. Maynard R.) Encyclopaedia Britannica Inc, Chicago. Volume 42

36. Care Ethics https://www.iep.utm.edu/care-eth/ (Accessed 23 February 2020)

37. Brenkert G., Beauchamp T. Ed., 2010 The Oxford Handbook to Business Ethics. Oxford University Press, New York

38. Rendtorff J.D. Ed., 2017, Perspectives on Philosophy of Management and Business Ethics, Springer International, Switzerland

39. Morgan J., How this CEO is transforming his 22,000 person company to focus on social purpose https://thefutureorganization. com/how-this-ceo-is-transforming-his-22000-person-company-to-focus-on-purpose/ (Accessed 7 March 2020)

40. Honoré T. 1987, Making Law Bind, Oxford: Clarendon Press

41. Chen J., ESG Criteria, https://www.investopedia.com/terms/e/environmental-social-and-governance-esg-criteria.asp (Accessed 15 February 2020)

42. Trillium AM, ESG Criteria for investments. https://trilliuminvest.com/wp-content/uploads/2016/09/ESG-Criteria-09.16.pdf (Accessed 30 March 2020)

43. Leo Laikola https://www.bloomberg.com/news/articles/2020-06-15/a-26-billion-investor-says-her-esg-bets-outperformed-in-selloff (Accessed June 2020)

44. Heffernan, M., Unchartered, Simon & Schuster

45. Ramirez, R., and Wilkinson, A., Strategic Reframing, The Oxford

Scenario Planning Approach, Oxford University Press, Oxford, United Kingdom

46. McKinsey's three arrows of time as explored in Ramirez, R., and Wilkinson, A., Strategic Reframing, The Oxford Scenario Planning Approach, Oxford University Press, Oxford, United Kingdom

47. Friedman Z., Why Millennials Leave their jobs https://www.forbes.com/sites/zackfriedman/2018/05/22/millennials-quit-job/#245c294057f1 (Accessed 15 February 2020)

48. Lauricella T. & Liu J., Four Lessons from Blackrock's Bold ESG Statement https://www.morningstar.com/articles/962317/4-lessons-from-blackrocks-bold-esg-statement (Accessed 2 February 2020)

49. Henizs W. Koller T, Nuttall R. Five ways that ESG creates Value. https://www.mckinsey.com/business-functions/strategy-and-corporate-finance/our-insights/five-ways-that-esg-creates-value, (Accessed 3 January 2020)

50. Henizs W. Koller T, Nuttall R. Five ways that ESG creates Value. https://www.mckinsey.com/business-functions/strategy-and-corporate-finance/our-insights/five-ways-that-esg-creates-value, (Accessed 3 January 2020)

51. Lauricella T. Liu J., Four Lessons from Blackrock's Bold ESG Statement https://www.morningstar.com/articles/962317/4-lessons-from-blackrocks-bold-esg-statement (Accessed 2 February 2020)

52. Thompson J., The FT Companies with strong ESG scores outperform, study finds, https://www.ft.com/content/f99b0399-ee67-3497-98ff-eed4b04cfde5 (Accessed 14 March 2020)

53. Denning S., The origin of the world dumbest idea https://www.forbes.com/sites/stevedenning/2013/06/26/

the-origin-of-the-worlds-dumbest-idea-milton-friedman/#3f506d72870e (Accessed 29 February 2020)

54. Kerry C.F., Why protecting privacy is a losing game today—and how to change the game https://www.brookings.edu/research/why-protecting-privacy-is-a-losing-game-today-and-how-to-change-the-game/ (Accesses 14 March 2020)

55. World Economic Forum, Global Technology Governance Summit, https://www.weforum.org/events/global-technology-governance-summit-2020 (Accessed 1 February 2020)

56. McCarthy M. Bitcoin devours more electricity than Switzerland. https://www.forbes.com/sites/niallmccarthy/2019/07/08/bitcoin-devours-more-electricity-than-switzerland-infographic/#434c8a2321c0 (Accessed 15 February 2020)

57. Data Centres Of The World Will Consume 1/5 Of Earth's Power By 2025 https://data-economy.com/data-centres-world-will-consume-1-5-earths-power-2025/ (Accesses 15 February 2020)

58. United Nations report Turn toxic e-waste into a source of 'decent work' https://news.un.org/en/story/2019/04/1036781 (Accessed 20 February 2020)

59. Chang A., The Cambridge Analytica Scandal Explained, https://www.vox.com/policy-and-politics/2018/3/23/17151916/facebook-cambridge-analytica-trump-diagram (Accessed 20 February 2020)

60. Read the declassified report on Russian interference in the U.S. election https://apps.washingtonpost.com/g/documents/national/read-the-declassified-report-on-russian-interference-in-the-us-election/2433/ (Accessed 23 February 2020)

61. Foster D. Deep Biases? Fixing AI's unintentional prejudices https://towardsdatascience.com/

deep-biases-fixing-ais-unintentional-prejudices-234893a40a3b (Accessed 23 February 2020)

62. World Economic Forum, Global Technology Governance Summit, https://www.weforum.org/events/global-technology-governance-summit-2020 (Accessed 1 February 2020)

63. English S., Hammond S., Cost of Compliance. https://legal.thomsonreuters.com/en/insights/reports/cost-compliance-2017 (Accessed 3 January 2020)

64. Kaminski P. Robu K., A best-practice model for bank compliance https://www.mckinsey.com/business-functions/risk/our-insights/a-best-practice-model-for-bank-compliance

65. Boyer S., We're all at risk when 65% of stressed-out cybersecurity and IT workers are thinking about quitting, tech exec warns, https://www.cnbc.com/2019/10/11/65percent-of-stressed-out-cybersecurity-it-workers-think-about-quitting.html (Accessed 27 January 2020)

66. ISACA, 2020, State of Enterprise Risk Management. (Accessed 28 January 2020)

67. Barth B., Data breaches expected to cost $5 trillion by 2024 https://www.scmagazine.com/home/research/annual-global-data-breach-costs-to-exceed-5-trillion-by-2024-report/ (Accessed 24 February 2020)

68. Townsend K., Cybersecurity Workforce Gap: 145% Growth Needed to Meet Global Demand https://www.securityweek.com/cybersecurity-workforce-gap-145-growth-needed-meet-global-demand (Accessed 3 January 2020)

69. Butcher D., Banks are engaging in a recruitment war for cybersecurity talent. https://news.efinancialcareers.com/

sg-en/276821/deloitte-banks-are-engaging-in-a-recruitment-war-for-cybersecurity-talent (Accessed 8 March 2020)

70. OWASP Top 10 https://owasp.org/www-project-top-ten/ (Accessed 26 February 2020)

71. Andersen E.S., Grude K.V., Haug T., Goal Directed Project Management http://citeseerx.ist.psu.edu/viewdoc/download?doi=10.1.1.473.7131&rep=rep1&type=pdf (Accessed 20 February 2020)

72. ISACA, 2020, State of Enterprise Risk Management. (Accessed 28 January 2020)

73. Jackson M. C., 2019, Critical Systems Thinking and the Management of Complexity.

74. World Economic Forum, Global Risk report 2019, http://www3.weforum.org/docs/WEF_Global_Risks_Report_2019.pdf, (Accessed 12 December 2019)

75. Polgreen L., The Collapse of the Information Ecosystem Poses Profound Risk for Humanity. https://www.theguardian.com/commentisfree/2019/nov/19/the-collapse-of-the-information-ecosystem-poses-profound-risks-for-humanity?CMP=share_btn_wa (Accessed 3 January 2020)

76. Fruhlinger J. What is Stuxnet, who created it and how does it work? https://www.csoonline.com/article/3218104/what-is-stuxnet-who-created-it-and-how-does-it-work.html (Accessed 23 February 2020)

77. Greenberg A., How an Entire Nation Became Russia's Test Lab for Cyberwar https://www.wired.com/story/russian-hackers-attack-ukraine/ (Accessed 23 February 2020)

78. Cavaliere V., Fung B., Equifax exposed 150 million Americans' personal data. Now it will pay up to $700 million https://edition.cnn.com/2019/07/22/tech/equifax-hack-ftc/index.html (Accessed 23 February 2020)

79. Jackson M. C., 2019, Critical Systems Thinking and the Management of Complexity. (p 201-226)

80. Jackson M. C., 2019, Critical Systems Thinking and the Management of Complexity. (p 227-259)

81. Jackson M. C., 2019, Critical Systems Thinking and the Management of Complexity. (p 263-289)

82. ISACA Launches Business Model for cybersecurity https://www.computerweekly.com/news/2240022960/ISACA-launches-Business-Model-For-Information-Security (Accessed 15 February 2020)

83. Jackson M. C., 2019, Critical Systems Thinking and the Management of Complexity. (p 263-289)

84. Jackson M. C., 2019, Critical Systems Thinking and the Management of Complexity. (p 291-340)

85. Ramirez, R., and Wilkinson, A., Strategic Reframing, Oxford University Press, Great Clarendon Street Oxford, UK

86. Madhav, N., Oppenheim, B., Gallivan, M., Mulembakani,P., Rubin E., Wolfe, N., Pandemics: Risks, Impacts, and Mitigation https://www.ncbi.nlm.nih.gov/books/NBK525302/ (Accessed 28th April 2020)

87. WHO Reports fivefold increase in cyberattacks, https://www.who.int/news-room/detail/23-04-2020-who-reports-fivefold-increase-in-cyber-attacks-urges-vigilance (accessed 1 May 2020)

88. Taylor P., Covid-19 themed cyberattacks hit healthcare bodies, https://pharmaphorum.com/news/covid-19-themed-cyberattacks-hit-healthcare-bodies/ (Accessed 1 May 2020)

89. Ramirez and Wilkinson prefer the TUNA acronym to describe volatility, uncertainty, complexity and ambiguity but on analysis it has an uncanny resemblance to VUCA.

90. Ramirez, R., and Wilkinson, A., Strategic Reframing, Oxford University Press, Great Clarendon Street Oxford, UK

91. ISACA, 2020, The NIST CSF Implementation Guide for COBIT 2019

92. Lockheed Martin Cyber Kill Chain https://www.lockheedmartin.com/en-us/capabilities/cyber/cyber-kill-chain.html

93. GitHub NIST CSF Excel Spreadsheet https://github.com/brianwifaneye/NIST-CSF (accessed 9 February 2020)

94. Honoré T. 1987, Making Law Bind, Oxford: Clarendon Press.

95. Warbuton N. 2007, Arguments for Freedom, The Open University, Milton Keynes, UK

96. University of Cambridge, Online hate speech could be contained like a computer virus, say Cambridge researchers, https://www.eurekalert.org/pub_releases/2019-12/uoc-ohs121719.php (Accessed 27 January 2020)

97. Aristotle, Defeat the Sophist https://en.wikipedia.org/wiki/Sophistical_Refutations (accesses 9 February 2020)

98. Jackson M. C., 2019, Critical Systems Thinking and the Management of Complexity. (p 291-340)

99. The Gaudian, Firms ignoring climate crisis will go bankrupt, says

Mark Carney https://www.theguardian.com/environment/2019/oct/13/firms-ignoring-climate-crisis-bankrupt-mark-carney-bank-england-governor (Accessed 24 February 2020)

100. With permission ISACA, 2019, COBIT 2019, Introduction and Methodology. ISACA, Shaumburg, USA.

101. With permission ISACA, 2020, The NIST CSF Implementation Guide for COBIT 2019

BIBLIOGRAPHY

The author deliberately set out not to write a book that will conform to academic rigour. In that, he was successful. The author wanted to avoid cluttering the text with references. However, below is a list of readings used in the development of this enquiry followed by some online readings, and courses that might be useful to anyone who wants to pursue this.

Aristotle. 282-324 BCE, Various readings including on logic, physics, metaphysics, defeating the sophist and ethics. Great Books of the Western World (ed. Maynard R.) Encyclopaedia Britannica Inc, Chicago. Volume 8 and 9.

Bentham J. 1748-1832, An Introduction to the Principles of Morals and Legislation

Brenkert G., Beauchamp T. Ed., 2010 The Oxford Handbook to Business Ethics. Oxford University Press, New York

Honoré T. 1987, Making Law Bind, Oxford: Clarendon Press.

ISACA, 2019, COBIT 2019, Introduction and Methodology. ISACA, Shaumburg, USA.

ISACA, 2020, The NIST CSF Implementation Guide for COBIT 2019

Jackson M. C., 2019, Critical Systems Thinking and the Management of Complexity.

Kant E. 1724-1768, Groundwork of the Metaphysics of Morals, Critique of Practical Reason and Metaphysics of Morals, Great Books of the Western World (ed. Maynard R.) Encyclopaedia Britannica Inc, Chicago. Volume 42.

Marinoff L. 2002, Philosophical Practice, Academic Press, New York.

Mill S. 1806-1873, Utilitarianism. Great Books of the Western World (ed. Maynard R.) Encyclopaedia Britannica Inc, Chicago. Volume 43.

Ramirez, R., and Wilkinson, A., Strategic Reframing, Oxford University Press, Great Clarendon Street Oxford, UK

Rendtorff J.D. Ed., 2017, Perspectives on Philosophy of Management and Business Ethics, Springer International, Switzerland.

Smith A. Great Books of the Western World (ed. Maynard R.) Encyclopaedia Britannica Inc, Chicago. Volume 39

Stewart M., 2009, The Management Myth, WW Norton and Co, New York.